pillsbury publications

Pillsbury's Creative Cooking In Minutes

Especially good and easy meals for all occasions

Also available from Pillsbury Publications:

Pillsbury's Family Cook Book
Pillsbury's Entertainment Idea Handbook
Pillsbury's Family Weight Control Cook Book
Pillsbury's Meat Cook Book
Pillsbury's Money Saving Meals

Pillsbury's Bake Off Cookie Book
Pillsbury's Bake Off Main Dish Cook Book
Pillsbury's Bake Off Dessert Cook Book
Pillsbury's Bake Off Breads Cook Book
Pillsbury's Bake Off Cake Cook Book

If not available at your local bookstore, please write to the following address: Pillsbury Publications, Box 1532, Dept. 256, Minneapolis, Minn. 55460.

Dear Homemaker,

Pillsbury Publications is pleased to present a cook book for people who like to cook and care about food but who don't have all the free time that they would like to have. Pillsbury's Creative Cooking in Minutes helps you serve a great meal in a short period of time.

Homemakers took an active part in designing this book. They told us that anyone could save time by opening a can or box and heating the contents . . . what they wanted were quick, creative food ideas that they could serve to their families with pride.

Following recipe development and testing in Publications' Kitchens, the recipes were given to homemakers to be tried again and served to their friends and families. Their invaluable suggestions assisted us in creating a completely usable cook book.

The recipes for this book were selected on the basis of their family appeal, nutritional contribution to the meal plan and ease of preparation. We have coordinated some of these recipes into menu suggestions. Each of the menus is complete, but you may want to use only part of it along with your old favorites or combine other recipes in this book into completely new menus.

Cooking for your family doesn't have to be a dull chore. We hope you find in this book all kinds of new ideas for creative meals that allow you to spend less time in the kitchen, yet serve your family praise-worthy meals.

Cordially,

Dianne Hennessy King

Dianne Hennessy King
Editor, Pillsbury Publications

Contents

Introduction

Tradition has it that the type of food Mother used to make when she spent all day in the kitchen is the best. Our families still love that food, but women's time responsibilities have changed since then. Most of us don't have all day to spend in the kitchen.

Creativity and quality are the marks of a good cook, and they are just as essential in convenience cooking as they are in cooking from scratch. No homemaker wants to sacrifice quality for a savings in time, and we don't think you should have to. The "Hey, Mom, what smells so good?" comments are ones we all like to hear. So, in order to maintain the "old fashioned goodness" but put it into the "today's woman" time context, we've developed recipes using new ingredients and shortcutted methods to achieve those great old favorite flavor combinations.

Many of the recipes in this book use ingredients which you have on hand or that you can keep on hand for spur-of-the-moment occasions. Others use new ingredients — some of which you may not be familiar with. Where possible, we've given ingredient alternates and substitutions to allow you to tailor the recipes to your own cooking style.

Some of the recipes here also use convenience products. The great timesaving advantages which are built into today's convenience products open up another avenue of creativity for homemakers. These convenience foods can, of course, be prepared as the package directs. But that's only the beginning. Convenience foods used as an ingredient, instead of as a final product, add another creative dimension to timesaving cooking.

You can also incorporate your creativity into meals through the variety of dishes which you serve. The recipes which you've made often and know your family likes can form a solid background against which you can inventively experiment with new dishes. We've taken the guesswork out of this experimenting by including recipes that are truly easy-to-do and have been rated excellent by many women and their families.

The variations of recipes you use, your choice of menu combinations and the ways in which you serve meals are your tools for imaginatively and nutritionally giving your creative best to your family.

To Make It Easier

Because the main dish is usually the most time consuming aspect of meal preparation, we've included a large number of recipes for main dishes — all of which can be prepared in about an hour or less. To help you get acquainted with these dishes before you make them, we've added introductory descriptions to the recipes. In addition to this, some of the recipes have been combined into sample menus.

All of the suggested accompaniments and the alternates are just that — suggestions. By knowing the particular food tastes of your family or guests you can substitute and rearrange the dishes to express your own individual kitchen expertise.

Time helps are given with each of these sample menus. In order to save the maximum time in food preparation and arrive at serving time with a relaxed attitude and a cool head, it's important to fix the individual dishes in a smooth-running sequence. The time helps are given for the particular dishes in each menu. If dishes that you substitute cook in approximately the same amount of time, you can still use the time sequence given. However, if the cooking times differ greatly, figure out a workable time schedule by using the approximate cooking times which are given with each recipe.

These approximate times are averages which were determined from the many tests which homemakers gave our recipes. It's generally true that the first time a recipe is made, it takes slightly longer to prepare than subsequent times when the method and ingredients have become more familiar. The approximate times can, however, be a useful guide in choosing recipes which will not only suit your menu needs but also the preparation time which you have available.

Each recipe also contains a suggested number of servings. These numbers refer to the number of average servings which the recipe makes — not to the number of people it will serve. Your knowledge of the appetite sizes of the people you are serving will interpret the number of servings each recipe contains.

In addition, we've found that most of the recipes in this book do not need any adjustment for cooking at high altitudes. Where a time range is given for simmering, it may be necessary to regularly use the longer time at higher altitudes. Other than that, any necessary adjustments are specified as HIGH ALTITUDE ADJUSTMENT and are included at the end of the recipe.

The ingredient variations and substitutions given within each recipe are designed to allow you to tailor the recipes to your own kitchen and cooking habits. In most cases, we've called for ingredients by their generic names — names by which foods are sold to grocers. If you do not recognize one of these names, your grocer can direct you to a brand name which is more familiar.

Kitchen Time Savers

Many factors determine the time it takes to prepare a meal. Naturally, the foods which you are fixing are some of the most important factors. In addition, the small amounts of time influenced by preplanning and organization are also valid considerations. Everyone's cooking habits and kitchen organization are different — in equipment, in space, etc. There are, however, a few guidelines that can add to time efficiency in any kitchen.

*Make sure you have all the ingredients before you start the recipes. Much time is lost if, half way through the recipe, it's necessary to make a trip to the store for additional ingredients. Whether you shop by the day or by the week, having all the ingredients before you start can save time.

*Start the recipes first which take the longest time to make (or which require cooling or chilling). Other components of the meal which are faster can be prepared in the remaining time, and the entire meal will be ready to serve simultaneously.

*When possible, cook or mix right in the dish you will use for serving. A variety of attractive dishes that can be used for both cooking and serving are available today. This can save dishwashing time, as well as free your kitchen from the clutter of extra dirty dishes. If you prefer to serve in different dishes, you can still help relax the kitchen atmosphere by washing some of the preparation dishes during spare minutes before dinner.

*Assemble all the ingredients before you start. Less time and energy is spent if you make one trip — as opposed to several — to the cabinets or refrigerator.

*Organize the equipment in your cupboards so that the items you use most frequently are closest at hand. Dishes or utensils which you use only occasionally can take a back-row seat and eliminate shuffling through the shelves for items used daily.

*Time and steps can also be saved if you store equipment nearest the section of the kitchen where you use it first. For example,

mixer bowls are usually used in conjunction with the mixer. You save energy by storing them near each other rather than having to walk across the kitchen to get one before using the other.

*Many convenience appliances are available for time-saving cooking, too. Blenders, pressure cookers, electric fry pans and saucepans, toaster ovens, and electric can openers are only some examples. If you have one or several of these, you will find that the more familiar you become with its operation, the more valuable it becomes as a time-saver.

If you know that the time you will have to fix dinner will be rather short, some of the preparations can be completed ahead of time — either that morning or the evening before. By doing some things ahead, you free more time at dinner for your family or guests.

*Chopped items, such as onions, green pepper, celery, etc., which you use frequently can be chopped in quantity ahead of time and stored, tightly covered, in the refrigerator.

*Desserts, gelatin salads, marinated salads, or recipes which require chilling before serving are convenient make-aheads.

*Recipe combinations which are mixed together and then baked can be assembled ahead of time and will be ready to pop into the oven when you start dinner.

*Meat dishes that simmer in a sauce can usually be made ahead of time and reheated before serving.

*The table can be set ahead of time, too — for a more liberated time schedule.

The main objective in time-saving cooking is, of course, to prepare delicious meals in the time you have available. But whether you spend all day or 30 minutes getting dinner ready, the meal will be a sure success if the food tastes good, is attractively served and the atmosphere is warm and friendly. Let the premium be on your time before dinner. Then relax at the table and make the most of the time that the family has together.

Appetizers

Teriyaki Strips, page 9, Aloha Crisps, page 7 and Chicken Pick-Up Sticks, page 9.

Refrigerated dough streamlines the time for these attractive and tasty hors d'oeuvres to just about nothing. Try some of the variations, too.

Approximately 20 min.
CRESCENT TWISTS

   1 can (8 oz.) Pillsbury Refrigerated Quick Crescent Dinner Rolls

   1 tablespoon melted butter or margarine

   2 tablespoons shredded Cheddar cheese

   Grated Parmesan cheese

   Garlic salt

Preheat oven to 375°. Separate dough into 4 rectangles. Press perforations to seal. Brush two of the rectangles with melted butter; sprinkle with Cheddar cheese and grated Parmesan cheese. Sprinkle with garlic salt. Place remaining two rectangles on top of seasoned rectangles. Cut each crosswise into ten ½-inch strips. Twist each strip 5 to 6 times; place on ungreased cookie sheet; securing ends by pressing to sheet. Bake at 375° for 10 to 12 minutes until golden brown. Serve warm.   20 APPETIZERS

> Tips: If desired, onion salt can be used for the garlic salt.
>
> For a flavor variation, sprinkle bacon bits over dough with the Parmesan cheese.

Approximately 45 min.
TANGY CHIPPED BEEF BALL

   1 package (1¼ oz.) horseradish dip mix

   ¼ cup dairy or imitation sour cream

   1 package (8 oz.) cream cheese, softened

   ¼ cup grated Parmesan cheese

   1½ cups (3-oz. pkg.) chopped chipped dried beef

In medium mixing bowl, combine horseradish dip mix with sour cream; blend well. Add softened cream cheese, Parmesan cheese and ½ cup of the dried beef; blend thoroughly. Set cheese mixture in refrigerator about 15 minutes to harden slightly for easier handling. Shape cheese mixture into ball. Roll ball in remaining 1 cup dried beef. Return to refrigerator; chill 15 to 20 minutes or until serving time. Serve with assorted crackers or chips.   1 BALL

> Tip: If desired, cheese mixture can be thinned with sour cream or milk to serve as a dip.

Approximately 15 min.
QUICK SPREAD APPETIZERS

   1 can (8 oz.) Pillsbury Refrigerated Quick Crescent Dinner Rolls

   ½ cup (4½-oz. can) deviled ham*

   ¼ cup sliced stuffed green olives

Preheat oven to 375°. Separate dough into 8 triangles. Spread with ham. Cut each into 3 small triangles. Top with olives. Bake on ungreased cookie sheet at 375° for 8 to 12 minutes. Serve warm. 24 APPETIZERS

> Tip: *If desired, other prepared spreads can be used for the ham. We especially like chicken spread and cheese spreads.
>
> If desired, chopped parsley or dill weed can be used for garnish.

A quick shake lends an exciting flavor twist to chips or other crunchy snacks. Good the next day, too.

Approximately 5 min.
MEXI-SHAKE SNACKS

   3 cups (7-oz. can) shoestring potatoes*

   1 teaspoon taco dip mix

In plastic or paper bag, shake shoestring potatoes in dip mix to coat evenly.

> Tips: *Potato chips or crackers can be used for the shoestring potatoes. Add seasoning by ½ teaspoonfuls to taste.
>
> Grated Parmesan cheese also makes a good flavor coating.
>
> Try other flavors of dip mixes, too, to make your own unique combinations.

Sweet and smokey flavors blend with crisp and juicy textures for these sensational treats.

Pictured on page 6
Approximately 20 min.
ALOHA CRISPS

   1⅓ cups (13-oz. can) drained pineapple chunks

   ½ lb. (about 8 strips) bacon, halved

Preheat broiler. Wrap one strip bacon around each pineapple chunk; secure with toothpick. Broil 5 to 8 minutes until bacon is crisp. Serve hot.   ABOUT 16 CRISPS

A lower caloried dip for chips or your favorite dippers — with a flavor that's compliment worthy.

Approximately 5 min.
CLAM DIP
1½ cups (12-oz. carton) cottage cheese*
¾ cup (8-oz. can) drained minced clams
1 teaspoon salt
⅛ teaspoon pepper
1 teaspoon lemon juice
1 teaspoon Worcestershire sauce
1 teaspoon chili sauce
Dash Tabasco sauce
Dash paprika

In blender, process cottage cheese at high speed, scraping sides of blender often, until creamy. Add remaining ingredients except paprika. Process at medium speed until thoroughly combined. Pour into small bowl; sprinkle with paprika. Chill before serving.
1¾ CUPS DIP

Tip: *Large or small curd, creamed or uncreamed, cottage cheese can be used.

"DIPPER" IDEAS
Potato chips
Tortilla chips
Crackers — plain or fancy
Melba or rye toast
Pretzels
Bread sticks
Shoe string potatoes
French fried onions
Specialty shaped and flavored snack-type crackers

Crisp vegetables, such as cauliflowerettes, radishes, celery, carrot and zucchini sticks, artichoke hearts, green pepper rings and strips, cocktail tomatoes, long green onions and cucumber slices are good served plain or with a dip. Prepare up to a day ahead and crisp in ice water until an hour before serving. Arrange on serving tray, cover and refrigerate until served. If desired, just before serving, sprinkle with a seasoned salt blend and serve with your favorite dip.

Approximately 5 min.
DEVILED HAM DIP
½ cup dairy or imitation sour cream
½ cup (4½-oz. can) deviled ham
2 tablespoons sweet pickle relish
¼ teaspoon Worcestershire sauce
Dash salt
Dash garlic salt

In small bowl, combine all ingredients. Blend thoroughly. Serve with chips or crunchy snacks. Store, covered, in refrigerator. 1½ CUPS DIP

Tip: To make in blender, combine all ingredients. Process on medium speed until thoroughly combined.

Approximately 45 min.
OLIVE CHEESE BALL
1 package (8 oz.) cream cheese, softened
⅓ cup chopped stuffed green olives
¼ cup chopped black olives
1 tablespoon instant minced onion
¼ teaspoon Tabasco sauce
¾ to 1 cup chopped parsley

In medium mixing bowl, combine softened cream cheese with both types olives, onions and Tabasco sauce; mix thoroughly. Set cheese mixture in refrigerator about 15 minutes to harden slightly for easier handling. Shape cheese mixture into ball. Roll in chopped parsley to coat well. Return to refrigerator; chill 15 to 20 minutes or until serving time. Serve with assorted crackers or chips.   1 BALL

Tip: If desired, cheese mixture can be thinned with sour cream or milk to serve as a dip. Use parsley as a garnish.

Olive Cheese Ball, above

Delicious teriyaki flavored meat that's rolled and baked in a flaky crescent. Easy to pick up and eat — makes great party food.
Pictured on page 6
Approximately 50 min.

TERIYAKI STRIPS

½ lb. sirloin steak, cut ½-inch thick

⅓ cup prepared teriyaki sauce*

1 can (8 oz.) Pillsbury Refrigerated Quick Crescent Dinner Rolls

½ cup (5-oz. can) drained, thinly sliced water chestnuts

Slice steak into ¼-inch strips. Marinate meat in sauce for 15 to 30 minutes. Preheat oven to 375°. Separate dough into 8 triangles. Cut each in half lengthwise. Place a meat strip and several water chestnut slices on each narrow triangle; roll up as directed on label. Place on ungreased cookie sheet. Bake at 375° for 10 to 12 minutes until golden brown. Serve hot.   16 APPETIZERS

Tip: *Teriyaki Sauce can be made by combining ¼ cup soy sauce, 1 tablespoon sugar, 1 teaspoon finely chopped onion, 1 crushed clove garlic, ¼ teaspoon ginger and 1 crushed bay leaf.

Approximately 15 min.

WIENER DAFFLE

1 package (⅝ oz.) Pillsbury Homestyle or Brown Gravy Mix

½ cup cold water

½ cup apple or currant jelly

2 tablespoons catsup

1 lb. (about 10) wieners or smokie links, cut into ½-inch slices

In medium saucepan, combine gravy mix and water; blend thoroughly. Add remaining ingredients. Heat, stirring frequently until sauce thickens and wieners are heated through. Serve with toothpicks for easy eating.
          8 TO 10 SERVINGS

Tip: Wiener Daffle can be kept warm while serving by placing in a fondue pot or small chafing dish. Ceramic or glass serving dishes, if warmed, will also hold the heat well.

A really great appetizer or snack that practically cooks by itself once it's in the oven. Good party food!
Pictured on page 6
Approximately 1 hr.

CHICKEN PICKUP STICKS

1½ lbs. chicken wings (8 wings)

1 egg

1 tablespoon cold water

⅔ cup finely chopped toasted almonds or peanuts

2 tablespoons flour

½ teaspoon salt

¼ teaspoon ground ginger, if desired

¼ cup butter or margarine, melted

Preheat oven to 375°. Cut off wing tips (reserve for making soup, if desired). Divide each wing in half by cutting through joint with a sharp knife. Combine egg with water. Combine almonds with flour, salt and ginger. Dip chicken pieces in egg mixture, then roll in nut mixture to coat well. Place in 13x9-inch baking pan. Pour butter over chicken. Bake at 375° for 45 to 55 minutes until deep golden brown and crisp. Drain on paper towel. 6 TO 8 SERVINGS

Tip: For an entrée, prepare with larger chicken pieces, increasing baking time to 55 to 65 minutes.

Wiener Daffle

Main Dishes

Chuck Steak Stew, page 15, Tomato Macaroni and Cheese, page 77, Braised Pork Chops, page 55 and Zippy Pineapple Baked Chicken Breasts, page 38.

Beef

Sauce mix speeds up these enchiladas (see Tip for sauce variations). Tortilla chips with avocado dip, and a vinaigrette salad are some of the traditional Mexican meal accompaniments.

Approximately 45 min.

EASY ENCHILADAS

    12 corn tortillas*
    1 package (1⅝ oz.) enchilada sauce
       mix**
    1 lb. ground beef
    2 tablespoons instant minced onion or
       ½ cup chopped onion
    2 cups (8 oz.) shredded Cheddar or
       Monterey Jack cheese
    ¼ cup chopped or sliced black olives

Preheat oven to 350°. In medium saucepan, prepare enchilada sauce mix as directed on package. In large fry pan, brown ground beef and onion. Drain excess fat. Stir ½ cup enchilada sauce into meat mixture. To assemble, dip each tortilla into sauce. Spoon about 2 tablespoons meat mixture and 1 tablespoon cheese down center of each tortilla. Roll into thirds and place seam-side down in 13x9-inch baking dish. When all tortillas are assembled, pour remaining sauce over top. Sprinkle with olives and extra cheese. Cover with foil; bake at 350° for 20 minutes until heated through and cheese is melted.

6 SERVINGS

Tips:*Frozen, canned or fresh tortillas can be used.

**Canned or homemade enchilada sauce to make 4 cups can be used for the mix.

For a milder sauce, use an additional 1 cup (8-oz. can) tomato sauce in preparing mix. Reduce amount of water used by 1 cup.

To save additional time, enchilada sauce doesn't need to be cooked before assembling enchiladas. Just combine ingredients and assemble; they'll heat during baking.

Meatballs take on a Hawaiian flavor with this sweet-sour pineapple and green pepper sauce. Serve with Chinese pea pods and a salad of cottage cheese on lettuce.

Approximately 40 min.

SWEET 'N SOUR MEATBALLS

    1 lb. ground beef
    ¼ cup dry bread or cracker crumbs
    ½ teaspoon instant minced onion or
       2 tablespoons finely chopped onion
    ½ teaspoon salt
    ⅛ teaspoon pepper
    1 tablespoon oil or shortening
    ¼ cup sugar
    2 tablespoons cornstarch
    2 tablespoons soy sauce
    2 tablespoons vinegar
    ½ cup water
    ½ cup reserved pineapple syrup
    1½ to 2 green peppers, cut into 1-inch
       pieces
    1¼ cups (13¼-oz. can) drained pineapple
       tidbits or chunks (reserve syrup)

In large mixing bowl, combine ground beef, bread crumbs, onion, salt and pepper; mix well. Shape into 1-inch balls. Brown in hot oil in fry pan. Drain off drippings; remove meatballs. Combine sugar and cornstarch in fry pan; stir in soy sauce, vinegar, water and pineapple syrup. Cook, stirring constantly, until mixture thickens and boils. Add green pepper, pineapple and meatballs. Cover and simmer 15 to 20 minutes. Serve over rice.

4 TO 5 SERVINGS

Approximately 30 min.

BEEF 'N WIENER BAR-B-QUE

    1 lb. ground beef
    ½ lb. wieners, sliced ¼-inch thick
    ¼ cup barbecue sauce
    ¾ cup water
    1 tablespoon sugar, if desired
    2 tablespoons dry onion soup mix*

In medium fry pan, brown ground beef; drain. Add remaining ingredients. Cover and simmer 15 to 20 minutes; serve over toasted hamburger buns.   4 TO 6 SERVINGS

Tip:*If desired, use 1 tablespoon instant minced onion and 1 beef bouillon cube or onion soup.

Burgundy flavors these meatballs subtly, and gravy mix makes the sauce especially easy. Rice, buttered green vegetable and a cool refreshing salad complete the menu nicely.

Approximately 40 min.

BURGUNDY BEEF BALLS

1 lb. ground beef
½ cup dry bread crumbs*
⅓ cup Burgundy or other wine**
1 tablespoon instant minced onion or ¼ cup chopped onion
1 tablespoon parsley flakes or chopped parsley
1 teaspoon salt
⅛ teaspoon pepper
1 egg
3 tablespoons oil or shortening
1 package (⅝ oz.) Pillsbury Home-Style Gravy Mix or Brown Gravy Mix
1⅓ cups water

In large mixing bowl, combine all ingredients except oil, gravy mix and water. Mix thoroughly. Form into 1-inch balls. Brown in hot oil in large fry pan. Drain excess fat. Reduce heat. Combine gravy mix with water; add to meat balls. Stir gently occasionally for 10 to 15 minutes, until meat is done. Serve with gravy.

4 SERVINGS

Tips: *Cracker crumbs can be used for the dry bread crumbs.

**If cooking wine is used, reduce salt to ½ teaspoon.

Dress up canned chili and turn it into a stew with these additions. Serve it with hot bread and a crisp salad for a hearty family meal.

Approximately 15 min.

CHILI CORN CARNE STEW

2 cups (1½-lbs. can) beef stew
1⅔ cups (15-oz. can) chili with beans
1 cup (7-oz. can) undrained corn with red and green peppers
2 teaspoons instant minced onion or 2 tablespoons chopped onion
1 to 2 teaspoons chili powder

In large saucepan, combine all ingredients. Heat thoroughly over medium heat for 10 to 15 minutes. Serve hot with crackers, chips or a hot bread.

4 TO 5 SERVINGS

Flavored crackers add flavor as well as crunch to these burgers. Baked beans, potato chips and a marinated vegetable salad would taste good with them.

Approximately 20 min.

ONION CRUNCH BURGERS

1 lb. ground beef
½ cup crushed onion flavored crackers
1 tablespoon oil or shortening
Salt
Pepper

Form patties from ground beef. Press cracker crumbs onto outside of burgers. Cook in oil in fry pan over medium heat until browned on both sides and cooked through. Sprinkle with salt and pepper. Serve as meat patties or in onion rolls as hamburgers.

Tip: Other flavors of crackers can be used for the onion. We've found bacon, cheese and sesame to be particularly good.

Gravy mix serves as a convenient base for a tasty barbecue sauce. Potato salad, buttered green beans and a tomato and cottage cheese salad are favorites with a meal like this.

Approximately 25 min.

BEEF BURGERS IN BARBECUE GRAVY

1 lb. ground beef
½ cup dry bread crumbs
½ cup milk
1 egg
1 teaspoon salt
⅛ teaspoon pepper
1 package (⅝ oz.) Pillsbury Brown Gravy Mix
2 tablespoons oil or shortening
½ cup water
½ cup chili sauce or barbecue sauce
1 teaspoon Worcestershire sauce

Combine ground beef, bread crumbs, milk, egg, salt and pepper. Shape into patties. Roll in dry gravy mix. Fry in oil in large fry pan until crisp and well browned. Remove from fry pan. Stir water, chili sauce and Worcestershire sauce into fry pan drippings; mix well. Add patties to sauce. Simmer 5 to 10 minutes. Serve patties hot with sauce.

4 TO 6 SERVINGS

Speedy Chili, below

A chilly weather favorite! Make it quickly with fast-blending flavors. Serve with a crisp refreshing salad and a fruity dessert.

The kind of dish that mothers used to make and families still love. Good reheated the next day, too. A tossed salad and hot crunchy rolls taste good with this.

Approximately 30 min.

SPEEDY CHILI

    1 lb. ground beef
    2 tablespoons instant minced onion or
        ½ cup chopped onion
    ½ cup chopped celery
    2 cups (1-lb. can) stewed tomatoes
    1¼ cups (10¾-oz. can) tomato soup
    2 cups (15-oz. can) kidney beans
    2 teaspoons chili powder
    1 teaspoon salt
    Dash pepper

In large fry pan, brown ground beef, onion and celery. Drain excess fat. Add remaining ingredients and mix well. Cover. Simmer 15 to 20 minutes, to heat well. Serve in bowls with crackers or corn chips.   6 SERVINGS

MACARONI GOULASH

    1 lb. ground beef
    1 medium onion, sliced or 2 tablespoons
        instant minced onion
    ½ cup (1 med.) chopped green pepper,
        if desired
    2 cups (two 8-oz. cans) tomato sauce
    2 cups water
    2 cups (6 to 8 oz.) macaroni
    2 tablespoons sugar
    2 teaspoons salt

In large fry pan or Dutch oven, brown ground beef. Drain excess fat. Add onion and green pepper; continue frying until tender. Add remaining ingredients. Cover; reduce heat. Simmer 15 to 20 minutes until macaroni is tender.   4 TO 6 SERVINGS

Tip: *For extra tomato richness, use 3½ cups (1 lb. 13-oz. can) undrained whole tomatoes or tomato pieces and 1 cup (8-oz. can) tomato sauce for the tomato sauce and water. Prepare as directed.

A simply super family dish that will become a favorite. Potato chips, relishes and your choice of a vegetable make it an easy meal.

Approximately 40 min.

BEEF 'N BEAN SUPPER DISH

   1 lb. ground beef
   ½ cup (1 med.) sliced onion
   ½ teaspoon salt
   ¼ teaspoon pepper
   3¼ cups (1 lb. 12-oz. can) pork and beans
   ½ cup catsup
   ½ tablespoon Worcestershire sauce
   2 tablespoons brown sugar
   1 tablespoon vinegar
   ¼ teaspoon Tabasco sauce

In large fry pan, brown ground beef and onion; drain excess fat. Add remaining ingredients; mix well. Simmer, covered, 20 to 30 minutes until flavors are well blended. Serve hot.

4 TO 6 SERVINGS

Very attractive and very tasty. Round out the color and flavor in this meal with broccoli and sliced tomatoes.

Approximately 30 min.

MEATBALLS ROMANOFF

   1 lb. ground beef
   1 egg
   ½ cup dry bread crumbs
   ½ cup tomato juice or water
   1 tablespoon instant minced onion or
      ¼ cup chopped onion
   1 teaspoon salt
   1 tablespoon oil or shortening
   1 package (5.5 oz.) noodles with sour
      cream sauce

In large bowl, combine all ingredients except oil and noodle mix. Mix thoroughly. Form into 1-inch balls. Brown in oil in large fry pan until cooked through, about 15 minutes. Meanwhile, prepare noodle mix as directed on package. Place prepared noodles over bottom of serving dish. Spoon meatballs on top of noodles. If desired, garnish with parsley sprigs or chopped parsley to serve.

4 SERVINGS

This quick and easy stroganoff is made with ground beef and mushroom soup for an easy and economical dish. Try serving with broccoli and a marinated salad.

Approximately 35 min.

GROUND BEEF STROGANOFF

   1 lb. ground beef
   ½ cup (1 small) chopped onion
   ½ cup (4-oz. can) drained mushroom
      stems and pieces
   1¼ cups (10½-oz. can) condensed cream
      of mushroom or celery soup
   ¼ cup water, red wine or beef broth
   ½ cup dairy sour cream or sour half
      'n half

In fry pan, brown ground beef and onion; drain well. Stir in mushrooms, soup and water. Cover and simmer for 15 to 20 minutes. Stir in sour cream; heat through, but do not boil. Serve over rice, noodles or chow mein noodles.

4 TO 5 SERVINGS

Tips: For an oven casserole, omit onion and spoon cooked mixture into a 1½ to 2-quart casserole. Top with French fried onions. Bake at 350° for 20 minutes until heated through.

Put these great flavors together in just minutes for a popular family supper. Coleslaw and a green vegetable make it a meal.

Approximately 20 min.

SOUTH-OF-THE BORDER SPECIAL

   ½ cup (1 med.) sliced onion or
      2 tablespoons instant minced onion
   1 lb. ground beef
   2 cups (1-lb. can) undrained tomatoes
   ½ cup ripe olives
   ¾ teaspoon chili powder
   1 package (⅝ oz.) Pillsbury Brown
      Gravy Mix
   1 package (6 oz.) corn chips

In large fry pan, brown onion and ground beef. Add tomatoes, olives, chili powder and gravy mix. Simmer 5 minutes. Serve over corn chips. Or, turn into 1½-quart casserole, top with ¾ cup crushed corn chips and bake at 350° for 15 to 20 minutes.   4 SERVINGS

Approximately 15 min.

BACON WRAPPED MIGNONS

  2 tablespoons butter or margarine
  1 teaspoon parsley flakes
  1 teaspoon instant minced onion
  4 beef tenderloin fillets, cut 1 to
     1½ -inches thick*
  4 slices bacon

Preheat broiler. In small saucepan, melt butter; add parsley and onion. Wrap bacon strips around outside of fillets; secure with toothpicks. Place fillets on broiler pan. Brush with butter mixture. Broil 3 to 4 inches from heat for 5 to 7 minutes each side for rare, 8 to 10 minutes for medium, brushing occasionally with butter mixture. Serve hot.   4 SERVINGS

   Tips: *These tenderloins are the same as Fillet Mignon. Boneless rib eye steaks can also be used for this recipe.

   If steaks are large, more than one strip of bacon may be required to wrap around each steak.

Approximately 1 hr.

CHESTNUT ROUND STEAK

 1½ lbs. round steak, cut ½ to 1-inch thick
   Meat tenderizer
   2 tablespoons oil or shortening
   1 pkg. (⅝ oz.) Pillsbury Home-Style or
      Brown Gravy Mix
   1 cup water
   1 tablespoon soy sauce
   ½ cup (5-oz. can) drained and sliced
      water chestnuts (Reserve liquid)
   Reserved water chestnut liquid

Cut steak into serving pieces. Prepare with meat tenderizer as directed on package. Pound meat with meat hammer or edge of saucer to tenderize. Brown well in oil in large fry pan. Reduce heat; add water and soy sauce. Cover; simmer 30 minutes. Combine gravy mix with reserved liquid from water chestnuts; stir into pan. Add water chestnuts. Continue simmering 10 to 15 minutes until meat is tender and sauce has thickened. Serve with gravy.
                     4 TO 6 SERVINGS

   Tip: If cover does not fit tightly, too much moisture may evaporate. If necessary, add small amounts of water to thin gradually after gravy mix has thickened.

Approximately 25 min.

SIRLOIN AND SHRIMP KABOBS

   1 lb. sirloin, cut into 1-inch cubes
   3 cups (12-oz. pkg.) frozen large shrimp,
      thawed
   ¼ cup butter or margarine
   ½ to 1 teaspoon garlic salt
   ½ to 1 teaspoon paprika
   1 teaspoon lemon juice
   Salt or seasoned salt
   Pepper or seasoned pepper

Preheat broiler. In small saucepan, melt butter with garlic salt and paprika; mix well. Stir in lemon juice (will be slightly separated). Thread beef cubes and shrimp alternately on skewers. Broil or grill 2 to 3 inches from heat, brushing frequently with butter mixture, for 5 to 8 minutes on each side until of desired doneness. Sprinkle with salt and pepper to serve.   4 TO 6 SERVINGS

Pictured on page 10

Approximately 1 hr.

CHUCK STEAK STEW

 1½ lbs. chuck steak, cut 1 to 1½ -inches
      thick
   Meat tenderizer
   2 tablespoons oil or shortening
 1½ cups (12-oz. can) beer or water
   1 bay leaf, if desired
   ½ teaspoon salt
   ⅛ teaspoon pepper
   2 cups (1-lb. can) undrained whole small
      onions*
   1 package (1½ oz.) beef stew seasoning
      mix
   4 carrots, peeled and halved
   4 potatoes, peeled and quartered

Prepare meat with meat tenderizer as directed on package. Pound well with meat mallet or edge of saucer to tenderize fibers. Cut meat into 8 to 12 pieces. Brown meat in oil in large fry pan or Dutch oven. Reduce heat; add beer, salt, pepper, bay leaf, onions and beef stew seasoning mix. Cover; simmer 30 minutes. Add carrots and potatoes. Continue cooking 10 to 15 minutes until vegetables and meat are tender.   4 TO 5 SERVINGS

   Tip: *1½ cups frozen small whole onions and 1 cup water can be used for the canned onions.

Salisbury Steak Menu

Salisbury Steak
Taters Terrific, page 105
Buttered Corn
Crispy Onion and Greens Toss, page 87
Beverage
Cinnamon Candy Peaches, page 114
MENU PREPARATION TIME: 50 MIN.

Approximately 45 min.

SALISBURY STEAK

- 1 lb. ground beef
- 1 tablespoon instant minced onion or
  ¼ cup chopped onion
- 1 teaspoon salt*
- ¼ teaspoon leaf basil
- ⅛ teaspoon pepper
- 1 tablespoon oil or shortening
- 1 cup (4 oz. or ½ pt.) sliced fresh
  mushrooms**
- 2 tablespoons butter or margarine
- 1 package (⅝ oz.) Pillsbury Brown
  Gravy Mix
- ½ cup water
- ½ cup red wine

In large mixing bowl, combine ground beef
with onion, salt, basil and pepper. Mix
thoroughly. Shape into 4 patties. Brown in oil
in large fry pan. Remove patties and drain well.
Pour drippings from fry pan. In same pan,
sauté mushrooms in butter. Add browned
patties to mushrooms. Combine gravy mix,
water and wine; add to patties. Cover; simmer,
stirring gently occasionally, 15 to 20 minutes
until meat is done.   4 SERVINGS

> Tips: *If cooking wine is used, reduce
> salt to ½ teaspoon.
>
> **If desired, use ½ cup (4-oz. can)
> drained sliced mushrooms for the fresh.

SUGGESTED ALTERNATES

Potatoes: Try Hearty Potatoes, page 104,
Quick Potato Browns, page 105, or Speedy
Baked Potatoes, page 105.

Vegetable: Any of your favorite vegetables —
maybe Bacon Fried Beans, page 97, buttered
peas, or Quick Orangey Carrots, page 100.

Salad: Something crisp and colorful — a lettuce
wedge with colorful salad dressing or your
own tossed combination, page 89.

Dessert: Make it fruity and serve it warm or
cold, according to the time of year.
Orange-Rum Baked Bananas, page 113, or
Peach Cobbler, page 113, woud also
taste good.

TIME HELPS: Prepare the peaches first. Then,
chill or let them stand and reheat them
quickly before serving. Fix the meat patties
next. Then prepare the salad greens while the
patties brown; chill greens in the refrigerator
until mealtime.

After meat patties are browned and mushrooms
are sautéeing, bring water for corn to a boil.
Cook the corn while the meat patties simmer.
Then, begin frying the potatoes.

Add the remaining salad ingredients and toss.
Then, everything's ready to serve — a meal
to please your family.

Try stew prepared a new way — with cube steak. Cooking time is reduced, and beef stew seasoning mix gives you all the stew flavors in one addition. Coleslaw and hot rolls are good meal mates.

Approximately 1 hr.

CUBE STEAK STEW

> 4 to 6 (about 1 lb.) cube steaks
> Meat tenderizer
> 2 tablespoons oil or shortening
> 2½ cups water
> 1 package (1½ oz.) beef stew mix
> 1 cup frozen or canned (8-oz. can) whole onions
> 4 or 5 medium potatoes, peeled and quartered
> 4 carrots, peeled and halved

Cut cube steaks in half. Prepare with meat tenderizer as directed on package. Brown well in oil (thorough browning adds rich flavor to gravy). Add water, beef stew mix and onion. Cover; reduce heat. Simmer 20 minutes. Add vegetables; continue simmering 15 to 20 minutes until vegetables and meat are tender. Serve meat and vegetables with the gravy.   4 TO 6 SERVINGS

> Tip: Round steak can be used for the cube steaks. Pound with meat hammer or edge of saucer to tenderize. Cut into pieces. Prepare as directed.

A dip mix provides an interesting and easy flavor variation for cube steaks. Try this one on the grill, too. Corn chips, a vegetable and coleslaw make it a meal.

Approximately 25 min.

WESTERN DIP CUBE STEAKS

> 1 package (.56 oz.) taco dip mix
> ½ cup water
> 4 cube steaks (about 1 lb.)
> 2 tablespoons butter or margarine, melted
> Salt or seasoned salt
> Pepper or seasoned pepper

In shallow bowl or plastic bag, combine dip mix and water. Place steaks in mixture for 10 to 15 minutes. Remove steaks from mixture. In large fry pan, cook steaks in butter 10 to 15 minutes until browned and cooked to desired doneness. Sprinkle with salt and pepper; serve plain or in buns. 4 SERVINGS

> Tips: Cube steaks can be broiled or grilled 2 to 3 inches from heat for 4 to 6 minutes on each side.
> For Mexican Dip Cube Steaks, serve with taco sauce or enchilada sauce.

Traditional Beef Paprikash takes a new fangled approach using cube steaks and sauce mix. Brussels sprouts and corn would be nice flavors to complete this meal.

Approximately 40 min.

PAPRIKASH BEEF

> 1½ lbs. (5 to 6) cube steaks
> 2 tablespoons oil
> 1 tablespoon paprika
> 1 teaspoon parsley flakes
> 1 teaspoon salt
> 1½ teaspoons instant minced onion or 2 tablespoons chopped onion
> ½ teaspoon garlic salt
> 1 cup (8-oz. can) tomato sauce
> ¼ cup water
> 1 package (1½ oz.) sour cream sauce mix

In large fry pan, brown steaks in oil on both sides. Drain excess fat. Add paprika, salt, garlic salt, tomato sauce and water. Reduce heat; simmer, covered, 15 to 20 minutes, stirring occasionally. Meanwhile, prepare sour cream sauce mix as directed on package. Add prepared sauce mix to meat and sauce. Stir in to blend well. Serve over noodles.
                5 TO 6 SERVINGS

> Tip: If desired, 1¼ cups (10¾-oz. can) condensed tomato soup can be used for the tomato sauce and water. Flavor will be slightly more tart, and sauce may be slightly thicker.

Minute Steak Lorraine

This streamlined recipe gives you the traditional sauerbraten flavor in a fraction of the time. Try serving it with potato dumplings and sweet sour red cabbage for a German meal.

Approximately 30 min.

MINUTE SAUERBRATEN

   2 tablespoons butter or margarine
   4 beef cube steaks
   Salt
   Pepper
   2 tablespoons chopped onion
   1 cup water
   1 package (⅝ oz.) Pillsbury Brown
      Gravy Mix
   1 tablespoon brown sugar
   1 tablespoon vinegar

In fry pan, heat butter; add meat and brown on both sides. Season with salt and pepper. Add onion; cook until tender. Stir in water, gravy mix, brown sugar and vinegar. Cook over medium heat, stirring constantly, until mixture boils. Cover and simmer 10 to 15 minutes until meat is tender.   4 SERVINGS

The flavors in this tasty dish will remind you of pepper steak; the method's much shorter, though. Tastes great served on rice along with corn and a fruity salad.

Approximately 40 min.

MINUTE STEAK LORRAINE

   2 tablespoons flour
   ½ teaspoon salt
   ⅛ teaspoon minced garlic
   ¼ teaspoon leaf oregano
   6 cube steaks
   2 tablespoons oil or shortening
1¼ cups water
   ½ cup (4-oz. can) drained mushroom
      pieces, if desired
   ⅓ cup dry red wine
   1 package (⅝ oz.) Pillsbury Brown
      Gravy Mix
   ½ green pepper, cut into 1-inch pieces

Combine flour, salt, garlic and oregano. Coat steaks with flour mixture. Brown meat in oil in large fry pan. Reduce heat. Add remaining ingredients. Simmer, covered, for 15 to 25 minutes until steaks are tender and flavors are blended.   6 SERVINGS

Flavored crackers add a subtle seasoning in the crispy coating for these cube steaks. French fried potatoes, buttered zucchini and a cottage cheese and fruit salad would be good with this.

Approximately 15 min.

CHEESE FRIED CUBE STEAK

   1 lb. (4) cube steaks
   1 teaspoon salt
   ⅓ cup crushed cheese crackers
   2 tablespoons butter or margarine

Sprinkle steaks with salt; press into cracker crumbs on both sides. In large fry pan, brown coated steaks in butter, cooking about 5 minutes on each side. Serve hot.
                                        4 SERVINGS

   Tip: Other flavors of crackers can be used
   for the cheese.

Parmesan Steaks
Hot French Bread
Skillet Fried Okra, page 101
Lettuce Salad with Italian Dressing
Beverage
Sherry Broiled Grapefruit, page 114
MENU PREPARATION TIME: 1 HR.

SUGGESTED ALTERNATES

Bread: Speedy Bread Sticks, page 108, or Noodles Alfredo, page 106, would taste good.

Vegetable: A green vegetable with interesting flavor, such as Confetti Beans, page 97, Orange Glazed Peas, page 101, or Spinach Elegant, page 102.

Salad: A crisp lettuce wedge, tossed greens salad, Caesar Salad, page 87, or coleslaw.

Dessert: Something fruity, for instance Daiquiri Peaches, page 113, Honey Lime Melon Balls, page 116, or Fruit Fondue au Rum, page 115.

TIME HELPS: The main dish takes longest to fix, so start it first. While it's baking, get the bread ready to go into the oven, and prepare the lettuce salad except for adding the salad dressing.

About 20 minutes before dinner, fix the okra and put the bread in the oven. While these are cooking, assemble the grapefruit and allow to stand until after dinner.

When everything's done, add the dressing to the salad and serve the meal. For dessert, broil the grapefruit quickly while you clear the table for a light and refreshing finale.

Approximately 1 hr.

PARMESAN STEAKS

- 6 cube steaks (1½ lbs.)
- ¼ cup grated Parmesan cheese
- 1 cup Pillsbury Hungry Jack Mashed Potato Flakes
- 3 eggs
- 1 clove garlic, minced
- 1½ teaspoons salt
- ½ teaspoon pepper
- ⅓ cup oil or shortening
- 1 cup (8-oz. can) tomato sauce with cheese
- ¼ cup grated Parmesan cheese

Preheat oven to 325°. Pound meat with meat mallet or edge of a heavy saucer. Combine ¼ cup Parmesan cheese with potato flakes. Beat eggs with garlic, salt and pepper in small mixing bowl. Dip steak in egg mixture, then in potato flakes. Brown in hot oil in a large fry pan. When both sides are well-browned, place in 9-inch square baking dish. Bake at 325° for 15 minutes. Add tomato sauce and sprinkle with remaining ¼ cup Parmesan cheese. Continue baking for 30 to 40 minutes until steaks are tender.   6 SERVINGS

Parmesan Steaks Menu

Flank steak makes an economical, flavorful steak, but should be medium rare to assure tenderness. Serve it plain or spoon mushroom sauce over slices. Complete the menu with potatoes, a creamy vegetable and a tangy salad.

Approximately 20 min.

LONDON BROIL

2 to 2½ lbs. flank steak
Meat tenderizer
¼ cup butter or margarine, melted
Pepper

Score flank steak on each side at 1-inch intervals. Prepare steak with meat tenderizer as directed on label. Place steak on rack in broiling pan and broil 3 inches from heat for 5 minutes. Brush with butter and season with pepper. Turn and broil 5 minutes longer until medium rare. Brush with remaining butter and season with pepper. Cut on the diagonal, across the grain, into very thin slices.

4 TO 6 SERVINGS

Tips: For garlic flavor, add clove of garlic to butter when melting.

The teriyaki sauce partially tenderizes this steak; cutting across the grain shortens the meat fibers and also adds to tenderness. Cook in the broiler or on the grill. Try serving with baked acorn squash, a crisp green salad and rolls.

Approximately 1 hr.

TERIYAKI GLAZED FLANK STEAK

1 flank steak (1 to 1½ lbs.)
⅓ cup prepared teriyaki sauce or marinade
⅓ cup water
1 tablespoon flour
2 tablespoons honey

Pierce steak generously with fork. In shallow bowl or plastic bag, marinate steak in teriyaki sauce for 30 to 40 minutes. Preheat broiler. Drain marinade into small saucepan. Add remaining ingredients to saucepan; mix well. Cook over medium heat, stirring constantly, until mixture thickens and comes just to a boil; remove from heat. Brush steak with marinade mixture. Broil (or grill over hot coals) about 2 to 3 inches from heat for 5 to 6 minutes on each side, brushing occasionally with marinade.

(For maximum tenderness, steak should be medium rare.) To serve, cut across the grain into thin slices.

4 SERVINGS

Tip: If desired, use ⅓ cup (5-oz. bottle) soy sauce, ⅛ teaspoon instant minced garlic, 2 tablespoons brown sugar, ½ teaspoon ground ginger, 2 tablespoons Worcestershire sauce and 1 tablespoon lemon juice for the prepared teriyaki sauce.

Meat marinade helps to tenderize the flank steak and shortens the cooking time for this popular dish. Try serving with summer squash and coleslaw.

Approximately 1 hr.

HURRY-UP PEPPER STEAK

1 flank steak (1½ lbs.)
Meat tenderizer
2 tablespoons oil or shortening
Dash pepper
1¼ cups (10-oz. can) beef consommé or broth
⅛ teaspoon garlic powder
⅛ teaspoon ground thyme, if desired
1 large green pepper, cut into 1-inch pieces
1 tablespoon flour or cornstarch
¼ cup water

Score flank steak. Prepare with meat tenderizer as directed on package. Cut across the grain into strips ½-inch wide. In large fry pan, brown meat in oil on both sides. Add seasonings and consommé. Cover; simmer 30 minutes until meat is tender. Add green pepper and continue cooking 10 minutes until green pepper is crisp-tender. Combine flour and water. Add to meat mixture and cook, stirring constantly until thickened. Serve with rice, if desired.

4 SERVINGS

Tip: One beef bouillon cube and 1 cup water can be used for the consomme, if desired.

The cooking time for this steak is shortened with the use of meat tenderizer. Try baked potatoes, Brussels sprouts and a salad with this savory tomato-flavored steak.

Approximately 1 hr.
SAVORY SWISS STEAK

- 1 to 1½ lbs. round steak, cut ½-inch thick
- Instant meat tenderizer
- 2 tablespoons oil or shortening
- 1 cup (8-oz. can) tomato sauce
- 1 tablespoon instant minced onion
- 1 teaspoon Worcestershire sauce
- Salt and pepper to taste

Brush or sprinkle instant meat tenderizer on meat as directed on package. In large skillet, brown round steak in oil on both sides. Drain fat. Add tomato sauce and seasonings. Cover. Cook over low heat 40 to 50 minutes, until meat is tender. Serve sauce over meat.

4 TO 6 SERVINGS

A pressure cooker makes this delicious steak a speedy dish. Turn it into a hearty meal with buttered peas, mashed potatoes and a carrot salad.

Approximately 50 min.
SPEEDY SWISS STEAK

- 1½ to 2 lbs. round steak, cut into serving pieces
- 2 tablespoons oil or shortening
- ¼ cup instant minced onion or 1 cup chopped onion
- ¼ cup chopped green pepper
- 1¼ cups (10¾-oz. can) tomato soup
- ¼ cup water
- ½ teaspoon celery seed, if desired
- ½ teaspoon paprika
- ½ teaspoon salt
- ⅛ teaspoon pepper
- 2 tablespoons flour
- ⅓ cup water

In pressure cooker, brown round steak in shortening on both sides. Add all ingredients except flour and ⅓ cup water. Close cover securely. Place pressure regulator on vent pipe. Bring cooker up to 15 pounds pressure or until pressure regulator is rocking slowly.

Reduce heat and cook at 15 pounds pressure for 15 minutes. Remove from heat. Let pressure cooker stand, allowing pressure to drop by itself. Combine flour and ⅓ cup water. Add to meat mixture. Return to heat and cook, stirring constantly until thickened.

4 TO 6 SERVINGS

Tip: Consult manufacturer's manual for instructions for your pressure cooker.

Versatility in this recipe lets you prepare it with minute steaks for a family meal or round steak for a more company-oriented dinner. Delicious flavors.

Approximately 20 min.
STEAK IN SOUR CREAM SAUCE

- 1 lb. tenderized round steak*
- ¼ cup flour
- ¼ teaspoon salt
- ⅛ teaspoon pepper
- 2 tablespoons oil or shortening
- ½ cup (4-oz. can) drained mushroom pieces
- 3 tablespoons chopped onion or 2 teaspoons instant minced onion
- 2 tablespoons water
- 1 cup dairy or imitation sour cream
- 1 teaspoon butter or margarine
- ½ teaspoon parsley flakes
- ¼ teaspoon salt

Cut steak into 4 pieces. Coat with mixture of flour, salt and pepper. Brown in oil in large fry pan. Drain excess fat. Add mushrooms, onions and water. Reduce heat; simmer, covered, for 5 to 10 minutes until tender. Add remaining ingredients. Heat thoroughly, but do not boil. Serve hot. 4 SERVINGS

Tip: *Four 4 oz. minute steaks can be used for the tenderized round steak. Prepare as directed.

Family and guests will enjoy these delicious flavors. Complete your meal with a crisp salad and cauliflower or green beans.

Approximately 1 hr.
CHEESY MUSHROOM ROUND STEAK

  1½ to 2 lbs. round steak
    Meat marinade
  ¼ cup water
  1¼ cups (10½-oz. can) condensed cream of mushroom soup
  ½ cup (2 oz.) grated Cheddar cheese
  1 teaspoon Worcestershire sauce

Trim excess fat from round steak; cut into serving pieces. Prepare with meat marinade, as directed on package. Drain marinade. In large fry pan, brown meat slightly on both sides. Reduce heat; add water. Simmer, covered, for 20 to 30 minutes, turning meat occasionally. Add remaining ingredients. Continue simmering, stirring occasionally, for 10 to 15 minutes until cheese is melted and meat is tender. Serve hot. 6 TO 8 SERVINGS

> Tip: If desired, golden mushroom soup can be used for the cream of mushroom soup, and cheese food spread can be used for the grated cheese.

Instant meat tenderizer and beer help this meat cook to tenderness in half the time, as well as give it a superb flavor. Serve this meal-in-one dish with a hot roll and crispy coleslaw.

Approximately 1 hr.
ROUND STEAK STEW

  1½ lbs. round steak, 1-inch thick
    Meat tenderizer
  1 tablespoon cooking oil
  1½ cups (12-oz. can) beer
  ¾ cup water
  2 packages (⅝-oz. each) Pillsbury Brown Gravy Mix
  4 potatoes, peeled and quartered
  4 carrots, peeled and halved
  1 teaspoon salt
  ⅛ teaspoon pepper

Prepare meat with tenderizer as directed on package. Pound with meat mallet or edge of saucer. Cut meat into bite-sized pieces. Brown meat well in hot oil in large fry pan or Dutch oven. Drain excess fat. Reduce heat; add beer, water and gravy mix. Stir to blend. Simmer, covered, 30 minutes. Add remaining ingredients. Continue simmering, covered, for 15 to 20 minutes until vegetables and meat are tender.   4 TO 6 SERVINGS

> Tip: For Zesty Round Steak Stew, omit water. Add 2 cups (16-oz. can) undrained small whole onions and 1 bay leaf. Prepare as directed.

Make Swiss steak with all the flavor and juiciness in less than half the time with a pressure cooker. Buttered peas, mashed potatoes and relishes would be good with this dish.

Approximately 40 min.
MUSHROOM BRAISED SWISS STEAK

  1½ lbs. round steak, cut into serving pieces
  2 tablespoons oil or shortening
  1 package (1¼ oz.) beef mushroom soup mix
  ½ cup (4-oz. can) undrained mushrooms
  ¼ cup water
  1 teaspoon Worcestershire sauce
  ¼ teaspoon garlic powder or ⅛ teaspoon instant minced garlic
    Dash pepper
  2 tablespoons flour
  ¾ cup water

In pressure cooker, brown round steak in oil on both sides. Add soup mix, mushrooms, ¼ cup water, Worcestershire sauce, garlic powder and pepper. Close cover securely. Place pressure regulator on vent pipe. Bring cooker up to 15 pounds pressure or until pressure regulator is rocking slowly. Reduce heat and cook at 15 pounds pressure for 15 minutes. Remove from heat. Let pressure cooker stand allowing pressure to drop by itself. Combine flour and ¾ cup water. Add to meat mixture. Return to heat; cook, stirring constantly, until thickened. 4 SERVINGS

> Tip: Consult manufacturer's manual for instructions for your pressure cooker.

The flavors that simmer with this round steak are terrific. Serve it as a family or company meal with mashed potatoes, glazed carrots and a tossed green salad.

Oyster stew lends mild and very subtle flavors to this simmered round steak. Great served over rice with snow pea pods and a refreshing fruit salad.

Approximately 1 hr.
SAVORY STEAK SIMMER
1½ lbs. round steak, ¾ to 1-inch thick*
Meat tenderizer
2 tablespoon cooking oil
1 package (2¼ oz.) cream of mushroom soup mix
1½ cups (12-oz. can) beer
1 teaspoon sugar
⅛ teaspoon ground thyme, if desired
½ cup (4-oz. can) undrained mushrooms

Prepare meat with tenderizer as directed on package. Pound with meat mallet or edge of saucer. Cut into serving pieces or smaller. Brown pieces of meat well in hot oil in large fry pan. Drain excess fat; reduce heat. Add remaining ingredients. Simmer, covered, 40 to 45 minutes until meat is tender. If sauce becomes too thick, add small amount of milk to thin as desired.   4 TO 6 SERVINGS

Tip: *Thicker cuts of meat will require longer cooking times for tenderness.

Approximately 1 hr.
BEEF IN OYSTER SAUCE
1½ to 2 lbs. round steak
Meat marinade
1 package (⅝ oz.) Pillsbury Homestyle or Brown Gravy Mix
1¼ cups (10½-oz. can) condensed oyster stew
¼ cup water
¼ cup sliced green onions

Trim excess fat from steak; cut into serving pieces. Prepare with meat marinade as directed on package. Drain marinade. In large fry pan, brown meat slightly on both sides. Reduce heat. Combine gravy mix, oyster stew and water. Add to meat. Simmer, covered, stirring occasionally, for 30 to 40 minutes until meat is tender. Stir in onions. Serve over rice.   6 TO 8 SERVINGS

Tip: For Oriental Beef in Oyster Sauce, cut meat into small pieces after marinating. Prepare as directed, adding 1¼ cups (7-oz. pkg.) frozen pea pods during last 10 minutes of simmering.

Beef in Oyster Sauce, above

Speedy Pot Roast
Hearty Potatoes, page 104
Dilly Green Beans, page 95
Peach Halves on Lettuce
Beverage
Eggnog Bavarian, page 111
MENU PREPARATION TIME: 1 HR.

SUGGESTED ALTERNATES

Potatoes: Try Speedy Baked Potatoes, page 105, Mashed Potatoes or any mashed potato variation, page 106.

Vegetable: Hearty flavors and bright colors are great here. Oven Browned Vegetables, page 99, Sherried Carrots, page 99, Savory Green Beans, page 95, or Creamy Peas and Corn, page 100, might be examples.

Salad: An easy tossed salad, page 89, or a fruit arrangement on lettuce, page 91.

Dessert: Something creamy, such as Quick Cheesecake Fix-Up, page 121, Lazy Grasshopper Dessert Pudding, page 111, or Vanutta Pudding, page 112.

TIME HELPS: Brown the meat, then cook it under pressure. While it's cooking, prepare the dessert and place that in the refrigerator to chill. Next, arrange the salads and place them also in the refrigerator until dinner time.

While the pressure on the pot roast is dropping, prepare the potatoes and vegetable. Thicken the meat juices for gravy, then ring the dinner bell for a hearty and satisfying meal.

Approximately 1 hr.

SPEEDY POT ROAST

    3 lbs. arm or blade-cut pot roast
    2 tablespoons oil or shortening
    1 large onion, sliced
    1 bay leaf
    ½ teaspoon salt
    ⅛ teaspoon pepper
1¼ cups water*
    2 tablespoons flour
    ⅓ cup water

In pressure cooker, brown roast in oil on both sides. Add onion, bay leaf, salt and pepper. Add 1¼ cups water. Close cover securely. Place pressure regulator on vent pipe. Bring cooker up to 15 pounds pressure or until pressure regulator is rocking slowly. Reduce heat and cook at 15 pounds pressure for 35 minutes. Remove from heat. Let pressure cooker stand allowing pressure to drop by itself. Place meat on a heated platter. Combine flour and ⅓ cup water. Add to juices in pan. Cook, stirring constantly, until mixture thickens and comes to a boil. Serve gravy with meat.

4 TO 6 SERVINGS

Tip: *For tomato flavored gravy, use 1 cup (8-oz. can) tomato sauce and ¼ cup water for the 1¼ cups water.

Speedy Pot Roast Menu

Wine Marinated Family Steak Menu

Wine Marinated Family Steak
Easy Potato Salad, page 92
Skillet Baked Beans, page 95
Sliced Tomato Salad
Beverage
Mint Whip Peaches, page 115
MENU PREPARATION TIME: 1 HR.

SUGGESTED ALTERNATES

Potatoes: Try a casual potato dish, such as Quick Potato Browns, page 105, or Quick Macaroni Salad, page 92.

Vegetable: Serve a picnic vegetable that's prepared simply — for example, corn on the cob, Pimiento Cheese Peas, page 101, Onion Simmered Beans, page 97, or Zippy Pork and Beans, page 94.

Salad: The refreshing flavors in Western Salad, page 90, or Citrus Avocado Salad, page 91, would team up well here.

Dessert: A cool fruit dessert, such as Daiquiri Peaches, page 113, Strawberries Deluxe, page 116, or Honey Lime Melon Balls, page 116, would complete the meal well.

TIME HELPS: If you plan to cook on the grill, start the coals first. Start marinating the family steak, then fix the potato salad and allow it to chill for a while. Prepare the beans next; they can simmer while the other preparations take place.

Put the meat on to grill or broil. While it's broiling, slice and arrange the tomatoes and fix the dessert.

This is a fun meal to serve buffet-style as a casual dinner for friends or family. Colorful paper napkins add a note of gaiety, too.

Cutting meat across the grain helps to make this less tender cut seem more tender. Longer marinating times will make steak even more tender. Make in the broiler or on the grill.

Approximately 1 hr.

WINE MARINATED FAMILY STEAK

    1 package (.7 oz.) French salad dressing
       mix*
    ¼ cup vinegar
    ½ cup red wine or Burgundy
    1 family steak (1½ to 2 lbs.)
    Meat tenderizer

In shallow bowl or plastic bag, combine salad dressing mix with vinegar and wine. Pierce steak generously with fork. Sprinkle with meat tenderizer. Place steak in marinade. Marinate, turning occasionally, for 30 to 40 minutes. Preheat broiler. Remove meat from marinade. Broil or grill 3 to 4 inches from heat about 10 minutes on each side, brushing occasionally with marinade. (Best tenderness is at medium rare.) To serve, cut meat across the grain into thin slices.   6 TO 8 SERVINGS

Tip: *Other flavors salad dressing mix can be used. Cheese garlic is one of our favorites.

A speedy fry pan variation on this delicious dish shortens the time you spend. Add buttered carrots and a quick gelatin salad to complete the menu.

Approximately 35 min.

SKILLET BEEF BOURGUIGNONNE

   1½ lbs. sirloin, cut into 1-inch cubes

   1 tablespoon butter or margarine

   ½ cup (4-oz. can) drained sliced mushrooms

   1 tablespoon instant minced onion or ¼ cup chopped onion

   ½ teaspoon salt

   ¼ teaspoon pepper

   ½ to 1 green pepper, cut into 1-inch squares

   1 package (1¼ oz.) beef mushroom soup mix

   1½ cups water

   ½ cup Burgundy or red wine

In large fry pan, brown meat in butter. Add mushrooms and onion; continue browning until tender. Add remaining ingredients except wine; simmer, stirring frequently, until sauce thickens. Add Burgundy; continue simmering for 15 to 20 minutes until meat is tender.

4 TO 6 SERVINGS

An herb butter mixture adds a new flavor interest to broiled or grilled steaks. Very easy to do in the broiler or on the grill. Some good meal accompaniments might be au gratin potatoes, green beans and coleslaw.

Approximately 20 min.

STEAK AUX HERBES

   3 to 4 tender steaks*

   ¼ cup butter or margarine, melted

   1 tablespoon parsley flakes

   1 to 2 teaspoons salad herbs or Italian seasoning**

   ⅛ teaspoon instant minced garlic

   Salt or seasoned salt

   Pepper or seasoned pepper

Preheat broiler. Combine butter, parsley, herbs and garlic; mix thoroughly. Brush steak with butter mixture. Broil steak according to timetable, brushing occasionally with butter mixture, to desired doneness. To serve, sprinkle with salt and pepper.

3 TO 4 SERVINGS

Tips: *Rib, T-bone, Porterhouse or Sirloin steaks can be used for the tender steaks in this recipe.

**Any favorite herb mixture totaling 1 teaspoon can be used for the salad herbs.

This very attractive and hearty mushroom-flavored dish is one that guests and family will enjoy. Snow pea pods and a fruity salad make nice meal accompaniments.

Pictured on cover
Approximately 1 hr.

BEEF AND MUSHROOMS

   2 lbs. sirloin steak

   2 tablespoons oil or shortening

   2 tablespoons instant minced onion or ½ cup chopped onion

   ¼ teaspoon garlic powder

   ¼ cup soy sauce

   ⅔ cup (4-oz. can) undrained mushroom pieces

   2 beef bouillon cubes or 2 teaspoons instant bouillon

   2½ cups water

   ½ teaspoon salt

   Dash pepper

   ¼ cup (4 tablespoons) cornstarch

Cut sirloin into thin strips about 4-inches long. In large fry pan, brown meat in oil. Add onion and garlic powder; cook until onions are tender. Add soy sauce, mushrooms, beef bouillon cubes and 2 cups of the water. Cover; simmer until meat is tender, 30 to 40 minutes. Combine cornstarch with remaining ½ cup of water and add to meat mixture. (Additional water can be added if sauce is too thick.) Cook, stirring constantly, until thickened. Serve over hot fluffy rice or noodles.

4 TO 6 SERVINGS

Tip: If desired, ½ cup (5-oz. can) drained and sliced water chestnuts or ½ package (7 oz.) frozen snow pea pods can be added.

Champignon Fillets

Even your most special guests will applaud these superb steaks. A potato casserole, buttered green beans or peas and a vinaigrette salad combine to make it an easy and excellent meal.

Approximately 15 min.
CHAMPIGNON FILLETS

- 4 beef tenderloin fillets, cut 1 to 1½-inches thick*
- 1 tablespoon butter or margarine
- ½ teaspoon salt
- ⅛ teaspoon pepper
- 4 slices bread
- ½ cup (4-oz. can) drained mushrooms
- ½ cup sour cream
- ¼ cup port, red wine or milk

In large fry pan, fry fillets in butter about 3 minutes on each side for rare, about 5 minutes for medium. Toast bread. Place cooked fillets on top of toast. Add remaining ingredients to pan drippings; stir to blend well. Pour sauce over fillets.   4 SERVINGS

> Tip: *These tenderloins are the same as Fillet Mignon. Boneless rib eye steaks can also be used for this recipe.

Dress up grilled or broiled steaks using this mild-flavored dip as a sauce. Artichokes, baked potatoes and a tossed salad make nice meal accompaniments.

Approximately 20 min.
T-BONE TRAFALGAR

- 1 package (1¼ oz.) horseradish dip mix
- 3 to 4 T-bone, Porterhouse or rib steaks
- Salt or seasoned salt
- Pepper or seasoned pepper

Preheat broiler. Prepare dip mix as directed on package. Broil or grill steaks according to timetable, basting occasionally with horseradish mixture to desired doneness. To serve, sprinkle with salt and pepper; top with extra horseradish mixture.   3 TO 4 SERVINGS

> Tip: For added flavor, 2 tablespoons chopped green onion and 2 tablespoons parsley flakes can be added to the dip mix.

Timetable for Broiling

Steak	Thickness	Approx. Total Cooking Time	
		Rare	Medium
Rib, rib eye or club steak	1 inch	15 min.	20 min.
	1½ inches	25 min.	30 min.
	2 inches	35 min.	45 min.
Sirloin, porterhouse, or T-bone steak	1 inch	20 min.	25 min.
	1½ inches	30 min.	35 min.
	2 inches	40 min.	45 min.

Steak in Sauce Diana Menu

Steak in Sauce Diana
Speedy Baked Potatoes, page 105
Peas with Crumbled Bacon
Waldorf Salad, page 92
Beverage
Strawberries Deluxe, page 116
MENU PREPARATION TIME: 45 MIN.

This steak is simply elegant served with its flaming sauce. It's easy to do — and ideal for company or special occasion since the flaming is even more outstanding in a candlelighted atmosphere.

SUGGESTED ALTERNATES

Potato: Double Tasty Potato Fry, page 105, Noodles Alfredo, page 106, or any potato casserole.

Vegetable: Choose a green vegetable such as Pimiento Cheese Peas, page 101, buttered broccoli, Caesar's Asparagus, page 94, or Dilly Green Beans, page 95.

Salads: Something cool and refreshing — maybe Fruit Slaw, page 91, Carrot-Raisin Salad, page 89, or Green Beans Tarragon, page 90.

Dessert: An elegant, creamy dessert. Try Light and Lazy Mint Whip, page 112, Mocha Pie, page 123, or Eggnog Bavarian, page 111.

TIME HELPS: Put the potatoes in to bake. Next, fix the salad and dessert; they can conveniently chill in the refrigerator until serving time.

Prepare the bacon for the peas and assemble the sauce for the steaks. Begin broiling the first side of the steaks and finish fixing the vegetable.

Heat the brandy sauce for the steaks and serve up the other dishes. Pour the heated sauce over the steaks and ignite.

The great flavors and elegant flame make this a splendid meal — suitable for any special occasion.

Approximately 20 min.
STEAK IN SAUCE DIANA

4 tender steaks*
2 tablespoons Chablis or sherry
2 tablespoons steak sauce
1 tablespoon chopped chives
2 tablespoons cognac or brandy

Broil steaks according to timetable page 37. While broiling, combine Chablis, steak sauce and chives in small mixing bowl. Warm cognac in small saucepan. When steaks are of desired doneness, spoon sauce mixture on top.
To serve, ignite heated cognac and spoon flaming liqueur over steaks.   4 SERVINGS

Tips: *Rib, Porterhouse, T-bone, Tenderloin or Sirloin steaks can be used in this recipe.

Cognac must be heated through before it will ignite. However, if heated too long, alcohol will evaporate and cognac will not ignite.

A great way to serve leftovers. Beef au Jus is great for sandwiches or by itself. Round out the flavors for this menu with sliced tomatoes, potato chips and a vegetable.

Approximately 10 min.
BEEF AU JUS
Cooked beef, cut into slices
Pan drippings from roast beef or 2 beef bouillon cubes*
1½ cups water
½ teaspoon soy sauce
1 teaspoon instant minced onion

Pour water into pan with beef drippings. Cook over low heat until bubbly. Add soy sauce and instant minced onion. Simmer 2 to 3 minutes. Serve over slices of hot beef. Beef slices can be reheated in juice and served over slices of crusty French bread.   1½ CUPS JUICE

Turn leftovers into a great meal with this flavorful stew. Hot bread and a crispy salad make it a great meal.

Approximately 40 min.
SECOND DAY BEEF STEW
3 cups (1 lb.) cubed cooked beef
2 cups (4 med.) carrot slices
4 to 5 potatoes, peeled and quartered
2 cups water
1 cup tomato juice
1 medium onion, quartered
1 teaspoon salt
1 package (1½ oz.) beef stew seasoning mix
2 beef bouillon cubes or 2 teaspoons instant bouillon

In large saucepan, combine all ingredients. Bring to a boil. Reduce heat; simmer, covered, for 35 to 40 minutes until vegetables are tender and flavors well blended. Serve hot.
5 TO 6 SERVINGS

Tip: For a flavor variation, use ½ cup red wine and 1½ cups water for the 2 cups water.

Barbecued Sliced Beef on Buns
Quick Macaroni Salad, page 92
Relishes
Beverage
Ice Cream and Jeweled Thumbprints, page 117
MENU PREPARATION TIME: 1 HR.

SUGGESTED ALTERNATES
Salad: Pantry Potato Salad, page 92, Easy Potato Salad, page 92, or a coleslaw would be good.

Dessert: Something casual and refreshing such as Minty Fruit Ice, page 119, or Orange-Rum Baked Bananas, page 113.

TIME HELPS: Start the cookies first, and after the first batch is in the oven baking, begin fixing the Barbecued Sliced Beef. The sauce for this simmers for a while — so you'll have time to finish baking the cookies and make the macaroni salad. Add the meat to the sauce. As it finishes cooking, prepare the relishes.

Dress up leftover beef roast with a spicy barbecue sauce. Great for a casual meal — be it family or friends.

Approximately 50 min.
BARBECUED SLICED BEEF
1½ cups (2 med.) chopped onions
2 tablespoons butter or margarine
1½ cups catsup
¼ cup firmly packed brown sugar
¼ cup lemon juice or vinegar
1 tablespoon dry or 2 tablespoons prepared mustard
1½ teaspoons salt
¼ teaspoon pepper
⅛ teaspoon ground cloves
1 tablespoon Worcestershire sauce
12 thin slices cooked beef
6 hamburger buns

In fry pan, sauté onions in butter until golden. Add catsup, brown sugar, lemon juice, mustard, salt, pepper, cloves and Worcestershire sauce. Simmer 30 minutes. Add beef; simmer 15 minutes longer. Serve on warm buns.
6 SERVINGS

Barbecued Sliced Beef Menu

Poultry

Your whole meal is cooked together in this recipe. Peas, sweet potatoes and chicken are topped with a very tasty peach syrup. Add a crisp salad or a relish tray for an almost effortless meal.

Approximately 1 hr.
POT O'GOLD CHICKEN
- ⅓ cup flour
- 2 teaspoons salt
- ⅛ teaspoon pepper
- 2½ to 3 lbs. frying chicken, cut-up
- ¼ cup oil or shortening
- 3 cups (1 lb. 13-oz. can) peach slices, drain and reserve 1 cup syrup
- Reserved 1 cup peach syrup
- 1 tablespoon instant minced onion or ¼ cup (1 small) coarsely chopped onion
- 2 tablespoons flour
- 1 to 2 teaspoons grated orange peel
- 1 teaspoon salt
- ½ teaspoon dry mustard
- ½ cup orange juice
- 1½ cups (10-oz. pkg.) frozen peas, thawed
- 2 cups (1 lb. 2-oz. can) drained syrup-packed sweet potatoes

In a paper or plastic bag, combine ⅓ cup flour with salt and pepper. Shake chicken in flour mixture to coat. In a large heavy fry pan, brown chicken well on all sides in hot oil (about 15 to 25 minutes). Pour reserved peach syrup over chicken and sprinkle with onion; simmer over low heat 25 to 35 minutes until chicken is tender. Combine 2 tablespoons flour with orange peel, 1 teaspoon salt and dry mustard. Add orange juice and stir until smooth. Push chicken to one side of pan. Pour orange juice mixture into pan; stir well to combine with pan juices. Add peas, sweet potatoes and peaches. Cover and simmer 10 to 20 minutes over low heat until peas are cooked.

4 TO 6 SERVINGS

Oriental vegetables and mandarin oranges add a light Oriental touch to this dish. Some interesting meal accompaniments might be a Chinese cabbage salad and green beans with almonds.

Approximately 45 min.
ORIENTAL CHICKEN
- 2½ to 3 lbs. frying chicken, cut-up
- ¼ to ½ teaspoon salt
- ⅛ teaspoon pepper
- 1 tablespoon oil or shortening
- ½ cup chicken broth or bouillon*
- ¼ cup soy sauce
- 1 medium onion, cut into wedges
- 1 tablespoon cornstarch
- 1 tablespoon sugar
- 2 tablespoons cold water
- 1 cup (11-oz. can) drained mandarin oranges, if desired
- ⅔ cup (5-oz. can) drained bamboo shoots
- ½ cup (5-oz. can) sliced, drained water chestnuts

Sprinkle chicken pieces with salt and pepper. In a large heavy fry pan, brown chicken in hot oil. Add broth, soy sauce and onion. Cover; simmer over low heat 35 to 40 minutes until chicken is tender. Remove chicken while preparing sauce. In small bowl or cup, combine cornstarch with sugar; stir in cold water. Add cornstarch mixture to pan, stirring until mixture thickens. Return chicken to pan. Add mandarin oranges, bamboo shoots and water chestnuts; heat through, about 5 minutes. Serve over rice.

4 TO 6 SERVINGS

Tip: *If desired, 1 chicken bouillon cube or ½ teaspoon instant bouillon and ½ cup water can be used for the chicken broth.

An easy orange glaze makes this broiled or grilled chicken very tasty. Serve it with your favorite accompaniments for a fun barbecue.

Approximately 45 min.
CITRUS GLAZED CHICKEN
  2½ to 3 lbs. frying chicken, cut-up
  Salt or seasoned salt
  Pepper or seasoned pepper
  ¾ cup (6-oz. can) frozen orange juice concentrate*
  ¼ cup firmly packed brown sugar or honey
  ¼ teaspoon ground thyme or poultry seasoning, if desired

Preheat broiler. Sprinkle chicken pieces with salt and pepper. In small saucepan, combine remaining ingredients; heat over low heat until sugar is dissolved. Broil or grill chicken 6 to 8 inches from heat for 15 to 20 minutes on each side, brushing frequently with orange mixture during last 5 minutes on each side. To serve, garnish with orange slices, if desired.
                    4 TO 6 SERVINGS

  Tip:*If desired, frozen lemonade concentrate can be used for the orange.

Try a variation on fried chicken with this savory coating. Potato salad, baked beans and other chicken favorites round out the meal nicely.

Approximately 45 min.
HERB FRIED CHICKEN
  ⅔ cup grated Parmesan cheese
  ½ cup (1 cup cubes) crushed herb seasoned stuffing mix
  1 tablespoon parsley flakes
  ½ teaspoon salt
  ½ teaspoon pepper
  ½ cup butter or margarine, melted
  2½ to 3 lbs. frying chicken, cut-up
  Oil for frying

In paper or plastic bag, combine all ingredients except butter and chicken. Dip chicken pieces into melted butter; shake 2 pieces at a time in crumb mixture. In large fry pan, fry coated chicken in hot oil until golden brown. Reduce heat, continuing to fry over low heat about 20 to 30 minutes until tender.   4 TO 6 SERVINGS

Snazz up the breading for fried chicken with onion dip mix. Add color and texture to your meal with a quick gelatin salad, a green vegetable and a potato casserole.

Approximately 50 min.
ONION DIPPER FRIED CHICKEN
  ½ cup dry bread crumbs
  1 envelope (0.56-oz. pkg.) dry onion dip mix
  ½ teaspoon salt
  ⅛ teaspoon pepper
  2½ to 3 lbs. frying chicken, cut-up
  Oil for frying

In a paper or plastic bag, combine all ingredients except chicken and oil. Shake chicken pieces, two or three at a time, to coat. In large fry pan, brown coated chicken in hot oil until golden. Reduce heat. Continue cooking over low heat for 30 to 40 minutes, turning occasionally, until tender. 4 TO 6 SERVINGS

Pressure cooker saves time in preparing this hearty dish. A large crisp salad or relish tray and a fruit pie for dessert make this a great cool weather favorite.

Approximately 1 hr.
EASY CHICKEN AND MATZO BALLS
  2½ to 3 lbs. chicken, cut into pieces
  1½ cups water
  1 tablespoon salt
  1 onion, sliced
  1 stalk celery, cut into pieces
  1 package (4½ oz.) matzo ball and soup mix

In pressure cooker, combine chicken, water, salt, onion and celery and soup packet from mix as directed on package. Cook as directed in manual for medium doneness. Meanwhile, prepare remainder of matzo ball mix as directed on package. Drop matzo mixture by tablespoonfuls into hot liquid. Cover. Simmer as directed on package (without lifting cover) until balls are cooked through. Serve broth in bowls with chicken pieces and matzo balls.   4 TO 5 SERVINGS

Prepared sweet-sour or barbecue sauce makes grilled or broiled chicken very easy to do. Brushing during last part of grilling time helps prevent excess charring of sauce.

Approximately 40 min.

EASY GRILLED CHICKEN

    2 to 3 lbs. frying chicken, cut into pieces

    Salt or seasoned salt

    Pepper or seasoned pepper

    ½ to ¾ cup prepared sweet 'n sour
        sauce*

Preheat broiler. Sprinkle chicken pieces with salt and pepper. Broil or grill 6 to 8 inches from heat for 15 to 20 minutes on each side, brushing with sauce during last 5 minutes on each side. To serve, garnish with pineapple or green pepper rings, if desired.

4 TO 6 SERVINGS

Tip: *Prepared barbecue sauce offers another quick variation. Prepare as directed.

This recipe combines chicken and a corn pudding mixture into one delicious dish. Complete this meal with a green vegetable, hot rolls and a crisp green salad.

Approximately 50 min.

CHICKEN 'N CORN SCALLOP

    2½ to 3 lbs. frying chicken, cut-up

    1 to 2 tablespoons butter or margarine

    1½ teaspoons paprika

    1 to 1½ teaspoons garlic salt

    ⅛ to ¼ teaspoon pepper

    1 cup (24) finely crushed saltine crackers

    ¼ cup butter or margarine

Corn Mixture

    ¼ cup flour

    ½ teaspoon salt

    ½ cup milk

    1 egg

    3⅔ cups (two 17-oz. cans) cream-style corn

    2 tablespoons instant minced onion or
        ½ cup (1 med.) chopped onion

In large fry pan, brown chicken in 1 to 2 tablespoons butter; sprinkle with paprika, garlic salt and pepper. Meanwhile, prepare Corn Mixture. Spoon Corn Mixture over

browned chicken. Reduce heat; simmer, uncovered, stirring occasionally, for 30 to 40 minutes until chicken is tender. While chicken is cooking, brown cracker crumbs in ¼ cup butter in small fry pan. To serve, garnish chicken with buttered crumbs.

Corn Mixture: In large mixing bowl, combine flour, salt, milk and egg; beat until smooth. Add corn and onion; mix well. 4 TO 6 SERVINGS

A pineapple glaze that tastes truly Hawaiian flavors this chicken while it bakes by itself in the oven. Great with rice, a green vegetable and a salad of crisp greens.

Pictured on page 10
Approximately 1 hr.

ZIPPY PINEAPPLE BAKED CHICKEN BREASTS

    2 lbs. chicken breasts (4 breasts)

    2 tablespoons butter or margarine, melted

    ½ teaspoon salt

    ⅛ teaspoon pepper

Glaze

    ¾ cup (8¾-oz. can) drained, crushed
        pineapple

    1 cup firmly packed brown sugar

    ¼ cup lemon juice

    2 tablespoons prepared mustard

    1 teaspoon soy sauce

Preheat oven to 375°. In an ungreased 9-inch square baking pan, place chicken pieces skin-side up. Brush with melted butter; sprinkle with salt and pepper. Bake at 375° for 30 minutes. Prepare Glaze; pour over chicken. Return to oven and continue baking 30 to 40 minutes, basting occasionally until deep golden brown and tender.

Glaze: Combine all ingredients; mix well.

4 SERVINGS

Tip: To prepare with:

Thighs: After glazing, bake 20 to 30 minutes.

Drumsticks: After glazing, bake 20 to 30 minutes.

Wings: After glazing, bake 10 to 20 minutes.

Chicken Cacciatori, below

A favorite from the old country! Colorful and full of flavor, this recipe saves you time through its quick method.

Approximately 1 hr.

CHICKEN CACCIATORI

3 lbs. frying chicken, cut-up
3 tablespoons oil or shortening
2 cups (two 8-oz. cans) tomato sauce
  with cheese
¾ cup (6-oz. can) tomato paste
2 tablespoons instant minced onion
  or ½ cup chopped onion
1 teaspoon salt
1 teaspoon Italian seasoning or oregano
¼ teaspoon garlic powder
⅛ teaspoon pepper

Brown chicken in oil in large fry pan. Drain excess oil. Stir in remaining ingredients. Reduce heat. Cover, and simmer 45 to 50 minutes until tender. If desired, serve chicken pieces with sauce over rice or spaghetti.   4 TO 6 SERVINGS

Prepared teriyaki sauce and an oven method let this recipe practically cook by itself. Try buttered French bread, a fruity salad and zucchini squash for an easy meal.

Approximately 1 hr.

CHICKEN 'AKI

2½ lbs. chicken, cut into pieces
½ cup prepared teriyaki sauce
¼ teaspoon butter or margarine

Preheat oven to 350°. Place pieces of chicken skin-side up in 8x8 or 9x9-inch baking pan. In saucepan, melt butter in teriyaki sauce. Baste chicken with sauce. Bake, uncovered, basting frequently, at 350° for 1 hour until tender. If desired, sprinkle with 2 tablespoons sesame seeds during last 10 minutes of baking.
                    4 TO 6 SERVINGS

Tip: For Sweet Chicken 'Aki, 2 to 3 tablespoons honey can be added to the teriyaki mixture before basting.

A simple but exciting tart honey glaze provides an easy way to give chicken new appeal. Try sweet potatoes, peas and a tart salad for interesting side dishes.

Approximately 50 min.

ZESTY HONEY GLAZED CHICKEN

2 tablespoons butter or margarine
¾ teaspoon salt
¼ teaspoon poultry seasoning
¼ cup honey
2 tablespoons prepared mustard
1½ lbs. chicken wings (8 wings)

Preheat oven to 375°. In a 9-inch square baking pan, melt butter. Add remaining ingredients except chicken; mix well. Dip chicken pieces in butter mixture to coat on both sides; arrange in single layer in pan. Bake at 375° for 40 to 50 minutes until tender and well glazed. For more flavorful chicken, baste once or twice during the last 15 minutes of baking.
                    2 TO 3 SERVINGS

Tip: To prepare with:
  Breasts: Bake 50 to 60 minutes.
  Drumsticks: Bake 45 to 55 minutes.
  Thighs: Bake 45 to 55 minutes.

Mashed potato flakes make a tasty and crisp coating for oven-fried chicken. A bean casserole, hot biscuits and coleslaw round out the menu for family or guests.

Approximately 1 hr.
TATER DIPPED CHICKEN
- ¼ cup butter or margarine
- 1 egg
- 2 tablespoons water
- ½ cup Pillsbury Hungry Jack Mashed Potato Flakes
- 1¼ lbs. drumsticks (6 drumsticks)
- ½ teaspoon salt
- ⅛ teaspoon pepper

Preheat oven to 375°. In a 13x9-inch baking pan, melt butter. In small bowl, combine egg with water; beat slightly. Place potato flakes in a pie pan. Dip chicken pieces in egg mixture; roll in potato flakes to coat well. Place in single layer in pan, rolling in butter to coat; sprinkle with salt and pepper. Bake at 375° for 50 to 60 minutes until tender and golden brown.

3 TO 4 SERVINGS

Tip: To prepare with:
Breasts: Bake 55 to 65 minutes.
Thighs: Bake 50 to 60 minutes.
Wings: Bake 40 to 50 minutes.

A simply great way to serve chicken wings (or any other pieces, too). Since the coating is crunchy and mildly seasoned, a creamy vegetable, a potato casserole and a fruit salad would be nice side dishes.

Approximately 1 hr.
SIMPLE SESAME CHICKEN
- 3 tablespoons butter or margarine
- 1 egg
- 2 tablespoons milk
- ¼ cup flour
- 2 tablespoons sesame seeds
- ¾ teaspoon salt
- ¼ teaspoon ground thyme or poultry seasoning
- ⅛ teaspoon pepper
- 1½ lbs. chicken wings (8 wings)

Preheat oven to 375°. In a 13x9-inch baking pan, melt butter. In small bowl, combine egg with milk; beat slightly. In shallow bowl, combine remaining ingredients except chicken. Dip chicken pieces in egg mixture, then in flour mixture. Place in single layer in pan, rolling gently to coat with butter. Bake at 375° for 40 to 50 minutes until golden brown and crisp.

2 TO 3 SERVINGS

Tip: To prepare with:
Breasts: Bake at 375° for 50 to 60 minutes.
Drumsticks: Bake at 350° for 40 to 50 minutes.
Thighs: Bake at 350° for 50 to 60 minutes.

A barbecue in the oven? Sure! And the biscuits are baked in the same pan. Complete the meal with corn on the cob and a marinated vegetable salad.

Approximately 1 hr.
OVEN BARBECUED CHICKEN 'N BISCUITS
- 2½ to 3 lbs. frying chicken, cut-up
- ¼ teaspoon salt
- 1¼ cups prepared barbecue sauce
- ¼ cup instant minced onion or 1 cup chopped onion
- ¼ cup water
- 1 can (8 oz.) Pillsbury Refrigerated Country Style or Buttermilk Biscuits
- 2 tablespoons grated Parmesan cheese
- ½ teaspoon Italian seasoning or ground oregano
- 2 to 3 tablespoons water, if necessary

Preheat oven to 375°. In ungreased 13x9-inch (shallow 3 qt.) baking dish, place chicken pieces skin-side down; sprinkle with salt. Combine barbecue sauce with onion and ¼ cup water; pour over chicken. Bake at 375° for 30 minutes. Turn chicken pieces; spoon sauce over chicken. Continue baking 10 to 15 minutes. (If necessary, add 2 to 3 tablespoons water to sauce to prevent sticking.) Move chicken to one end of pan; spoon sauce over chicken. Dip biscuits in sauce; place sauce-side up in opposite end of pan. Combine Parmesan cheese with Italian seasoning; sprinkle over biscuits. Return to oven and continue baking for 15 to 20 minutes until biscuits are brown. 4 TO 6 SERVINGS

The flavor and glory of fried chicken without the time it takes you to watch it in the fry pan. Bake squash in the oven at the same time, and add a green vegetable and Waldorf salad for a great dinner.

Approximately 1 hr.
GOLDEN OVEN-FRIED CHICKEN
   ¾ cup dry bread crumbs
   ¼ cup grated Parmesan cheese
   ¼ cup finely chopped blanched almonds, if desired
   2 tablespoons minced parsley
   1 teaspoon salt
   ¼ teaspoon ground thyme
   ⅛ teaspoon pepper
   ½ cup butter or margarine
   ½ teaspoon garlic powder or 1 clove garlic, crushed
   2½ to 3 lbs. frying chicken, cut-up

Preheat oven to 375°. In a pie pan, combine crumbs, cheese, almonds, parsley, salt, thyme and pepper. In an ungreased 13x9-inch (shallow 3 qt.) baking dish, melt butter with garlic powder. Dip chicken pieces in garlic-butter, then in crumb mixture. Place in baking dish skin-side up. Bake, uncovered, at 375° for 55 to 65 minutes until chicken is tender. (Do not turn chicken pieces during baking.)
                                    4 TO 6 SERVINGS

The magnificent flavors that ham, cheese and tomatoes give this chicken are the reason for its name. A recipe that's sure to win you fame. Interesting side dishes might include broccoli and a salad with tart flavors.

Approximately 50 min.
CHICKEN MAGNIFICO
   ¼ cup flour
   1 teaspoon paprika
   ½ teaspoon salt
   ⅛ teaspoon pepper
   2½ to 3 lbs. frying chicken, cut-up
   ¼ cup cooking oil or shortening
   ¾ cup (4 oz.) cubed, cooked ham (½-inch cubes)
   2½ cups (two 10¾-oz. cans) condensed Cheddar cheese soup
   1 cup (8-oz. can) stewed tomatoes

   ¼ cup instant minced onion or 1 cup (1 large) finely chopped onion
   1 teaspoon basil leaves

In paper or plastic bag, combine flour, paprika, salt and pepper. Shake chicken, 2 pieces at a time, in flour mixture. In large heavy fry pan, brown chicken well in hot oil, about 10 minutes on each side. Combine remaining ingredients. Add to chicken. Cook, covered, over medium heat 30 to 35 minutes until chicken is tender. Remove cover; continue cooking until sauce is of desired consistency. If desired, serve over rice or noodles.   4 TO 6 SERVINGS

Easy ingredients combine to make a sensational sauce. Make it a complete meal with Brussels sprouts, mashed potatoes and a marinated salad.

Approximately 1 hr.
NICE 'N EASY CHICKEN BAKE
   2 tablespoons butter or margarine
   ½ cup dry bread crumbs
   ¼ teaspoon salt
   ⅛ teaspoon pepper
   2 lbs. chicken breasts or thighs (4 halves)

Sauce
   1¼ cups (10½-oz. can) condensed cream of mushroom soup
   ⅔ cup dairy or imitation sour cream
   ⅓ cup dry sherry or sauterne

Preheat oven to 375°. In a 9-inch square (shallow 2 qt.) baking dish, melt butter. In pie pan, combine crumbs with salt and pepper. Dip chicken pieces in butter; roll in crumb mixture to coat lightly. Place chicken pieces skin-side up in baking dish. Bake at 375° for 50 to 60 minutes until tender and golden brown. Meanwhile, prepare Sauce. To serve, pour half of hot Sauce over chicken to coat well. Serve remaining Sauce in bowl.

Sauce: Combine soup with sour cream. Mix well. Gradually add sherry. Mix until smooth. Heat thoroughly.   4 SERVINGS

Chicken and Dressing Bake
Squash Vermont, page 102
Creamy Peas and Corn, page 100
Quick Filled Pears, page 91
Beverage
Mincemeat Ice Cream, page 119
MENU PREPARATION TIME: 1 HR.

SUGGESTED ALTERNATES

Vegetables: A hearty colorful vegetable, such as sweet potatoes or squash, and a light-flavored green one, such as beans or peas.

Salad: Something light and fruity, such as Fruit Slaw, page 91, or Carrot Orange Toss, page 90.

Dessert: A traditional-flavored favorite like Pumpkin Pie Cake, page 120.

TIME HELPS: Prepare the squash and place it in the oven to start baking while the chicken is browning. Then, place the assembled chicken dish in the oven to bake along with the squash. Combine the dessert and allow it to refreeze until after the meal.

Fill pear halves and arrange in individual serving dishes; chill them in the refrigerator until serving time. About 10 minutes before serving, prepare the vegetable. When all is completed, you'll have the traditional flavors of a chicken and dressing dinner in about an hour.

Tastes like a roasted chicken with dressing but takes much less time — old fashioned flavors with new fashioned convenience. A versatile dish that's appetizing for family or holiday menus.

Approximately 1 hr.
CHICKEN AND DRESSING BAKE

¼ cup flour
1 teaspoon salt
½ teaspoon paprika
⅛ teaspoon pepper
1¾ lbs. chicken thighs (5 thighs)
2 to 4 tablespoons oil or shortening
1½ cups (3 stalks) chopped celery
¼ cup instant minced onion or ½ cup chopped onion
7 cups (7 or 7½-oz. pkg.) seasoned bread stuffing cubes*
1¼ cups (10½-oz. can) condensed cream of chicken soup
1½ cups water

Preheat oven to 375°. In a paper or plastic bag, combine flour with salt, paprika and pepper. Shake chicken pieces, two or three at a time, to coat. In large heavy fry pan over medium heat, brown chicken pieces well in hot oil. Sprinkle celery and onion evenly in a 13x9-inch (shallow 3 qt.) baking dish. Top with stuffing cubes. In medium mixing bowl, thoroughly combine soup with water. Pour soup mixture evenly over stuffing cubes. Arrange chicken pieces over all. Cover tightly with foil. Bake at 375° for 45 to 55 minutes until chicken is tender. (For a drier dressing, remove foil the last 10 minutes of baking.)   3 TO 5 SERVINGS

Tip: *Since the amount of seasoning varies with the brand of stuffing mix, you may wish to add ¼ to ½ teaspoon poultry seasoning or thyme to increase the seasoning level.

To prepare with:
Breasts: Bake 60 to 70 minutes.
Drumsticks: Bake 55 to 65 minutes.
Wings: Bake 55 to 65 minutes.

Chicken and Dressing Bake Menu

Orange Chicken and Burgundy Menu

Orange Chicken and Burgundy
Quick Almond Currant Rice, page 107
Buttered Spinach
Tossed Salad, page 89
Beverage
Mocha Pie, page 123
MENU PREPARATION TIME: 1 HR.

SUGGESTED ALTERNATES

Rice: A mild flavored rice dish like brown rice, rice pilaf or fried rice.

Vegetable: Any green vegetable. Onion Simmered Beans, page 97, or Savory Green Beans, page 95 would be good.

Salad: Something with tart flavors and a little crispiness like Crispy Onions and Greens Toss, page 87, or any tossed salad combination.

Dessert: Light flavors and creamy textures, such as Choco Mint Pudding, page 112, or Pistachio Cream Tartlets, page 121.

TIME HELPS: Start the chicken first. While it simmers, prepare Mocha Pie and allow that to chill until dessert time. Next make the rice; and while that's simmering, cook the artichokes and assemble the salad.

By the time the rice, vegetable and salad are ready, the chicken will be finished, too — so place them in serving dishes and summon your family or guests for a very tasty meal.

An elegant tasting dish that's conveniently done in a fry pan — great looking, too. It's sure to win compliments for you.

Approximately 50 min.
ORANGE CHICKEN AND BURGUNDY

2½ to 3 lbs. frying chicken, cut-up
  2 tablespoons butter or margarine, melted
½ teaspoon seasoned salt blend or salt
⅛ teaspoon pepper, if desired
  3 tablespoons brown sugar
  1 tablespoon cornstarch
¼ teaspoon salt
⅛ teaspoon ground ginger, if desired
⅓ cup orange marmalade
⅓ cup orange juice
  1 teaspoon lemon juice
⅓ cup Burgundy*
  1 orange, thinly sliced, if desired

In large fry pan, brown chicken in butter. Season with salt and pepper. Add remaining ingredients, except Burgundy and orange slices. Reduce heat; cover. Simmer, stirring occasionally, 25 to 35 minutes until tender. Add Burgundy and orange slices. Continue simmering 10 minutes. Serve hot.

4 TO 6 SERVINGS

Tip: *One third cup additional orange juice can be used for the Burgundy. Increase lemon juice to 1 tablespoon; prepare as directed.

Chicken livers are fit for a king in this speedy recipe. A mild flavored green vegetable, such as beans, and a sliced tomato salad would be great side dishes for this meal.

Approximately 20 min.

CHICKEN LIVERS STROGANOFF

    1 package (12 oz.) chicken livers
    2 tablespoons butter or margarine
    ½ teaspoon ground oregano
    ½ teaspoon Worcestershire sauce
    2 tablespoons flour
    2 tablespoons instant minced onion or
       ⅓ cup (1 small) chopped onion
    ½ teaspoon salt
    ⅛ teaspoon pepper
    ⅔ cup (4-oz. can) undrained mushroom
       stems and pieces
    ¼ cup dairy or imitation sour cream

Cut livers in half. In large fry pan, heat butter with oregano and Worcestershire sauce. Add livers and brown slowly over medium heat for 5 to 7 minutes. Remove livers from pan; set aside. Blend in flour, onion, salt, pepper and mushroom liquid. Heat, stirring constantly, until mixture comes to a boil. Return livers to pan; add mushrooms. Cover and simmer 3 to 5 minutes. Stir about ⅓ cup of the liver mixture into the sour cream; add sour cream mixture to pan, mixing well. Heat through but do not boil. If desired, serve over cooked rice.

                                      3 TO 4 SERVINGS

A great recipe for chicken liver lovers. Delicious with a crisp salad, creamy vegetable and fried potatoes as meal accompaniments.

Approximately 35 min.

CHICKEN LIVERS WITH BACON CRISPS

    6 to 8 slices bacon
    ¼ cup flour
    1 teaspoon salt
    ½ teaspoon paprika
    ⅛ teaspoon pepper
    1 package (12 oz.) chicken livers
    3 to 4 slices bread, toasted

Preheat oven to 400°. *Place bacon slices in single layer on broiler rack. Bake 10 to 15 minutes until crisp. Remove rack and bacon; keep bacon warm. In a pie pan, combine flour with salt, paprika and pepper. Roll chicken livers in flour mixture to coat well. Place in hot drippings in broiler pan. Bake at 400° for 10 minutes; turn and continue to bake 8 to 10 minutes until browned. Drain on paper towel. Toast bread; lightly brush with bacon drippings. Arrange livers on toast. Criss-cross bacon slices over liver to serve. 3 TO 4 SERVINGS

    Tip: *If desired, bacon can be fried in fry pan until crisp. Fry coated chicken livers in bacon drippings for 15 to 20 minutes until lightly browned. Serve as directed.

Broiling is a speedy way to fix chicken; and because chicken is low in fat, there's very little spattering in your broiler. This one is fun on the grill, too.

Approximately 35 min.

LEMON BROILED CHICKEN

    2½ to 3 lbs. frying chicken, cut-up
    1 lemon, halved*
    1 teaspoon salt
    ½ teaspoon paprika
    ⅛ teaspoon pepper
    2 tablespoons butter or margarine,
       melted
    1 teaspoon sugar, if desired

Preheat broiler. Rub chicken pieces on all sides with cut surface of lemon, squeezing lemon halves to release juice. Place chicken pieces skin-side down on broiler pan. Combine salt with paprika and pepper. Brush chicken with half of melted butter; sprinkle with half of seasoning mixture. Broil or grill 6 to 8 inches from heat for 15 to 20 minutes until deep golden brown. Turn chicken; brush with remaining butter and sprinkle with remaining seasoning mixture. Continue broiling 10 to 15 minutes until chicken is tender and deep golden brown. For a special flavor treat, sprinkle chicken pieces with sugar about 3 minutes before end of broiling time.

                                      4 TO 6 SERVINGS

    Tip: *Three to four tablespoons bottled lemon juice can be substituted for the fresh lemon. Brush on chicken and proceed as directed.

The cooking time for this chicken is cut in half because the breasts have been boned. This exceptional combination of flavors would go well with a Caesar salad, summer squash and baked potato.

Approximately 50 min.
CHICKEN TIPPERARY

    4 whole chicken breasts, boned
    8 slices Canadian-style bacon
    4 tablespoons butter or margarine
    2 eggs, slightly beaten
    2 tablespoons water
    1 teaspoon onion salt
    ¼ teaspoon pepper
    1 cup Pillsbury Hungry Jack Mashed
        Potato Flakes
    Oil for frying

Cut chicken breasts in half; remove skin. Flatten each, using a meat mallet, until large enough to cover bacon slice. (To prevent breasts from tearing when pounding, cover with several layers of waxer paper.) Place slice of bacon, 1 tablespoon butter and second bacon slice on each half of chicken breast. Top with second breast half. Secure with wooden picks or strings. Repeat to make 4 servings. Combine eggs, water, onion salt and pepper in small shallow bowl. Dip chicken breasts in egg mixture; roll in potato flakes until well coated. Brown in oil in large fry pan about 14 minutes over medium heat. Turn and brown second side about 15 minutes.

4 SERVINGS

Tip: For an interesting flavor variation, place a slice of Swiss cheese between the Canadian bacon slices.

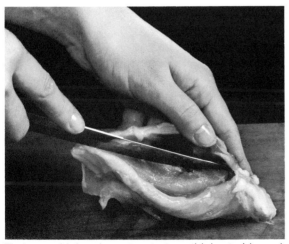

To bone chicken breasts, start on thickest side and cut along bone to release meat.

Hearty flavors and varied textures make this a popular recipe. Your time is free while it bakes. Summer squash and a green salad would make nice meal accompaniments.

Approximately 1 hr.
PIONEER TURKEY CASSEROLE

    1 package (6 oz.) wild rice mix
    2 to 3 cups cubed turkey
    ½ cup (1 stalk) finely chopped celery
    ½ cup (5-oz. can) drained and sliced water
        chestnuts, if desired
    ¼ cup diced roasted almonds, if desired
    1 teaspoon instant minced onion
        or 2 tablespoons chopped onion
    1¼ cups (10½-oz. can) cream of chicken
        soup*
    ⅔ cup (4-oz. can) undrained mushroom
        pieces
    1 cup water
    1 teaspoon Worcestershire sauce,
        if desired

Preheat oven to 375°. In large mixing bowl, combine rice mix, turkey, celery, water chestnuts, almonds and onion. In small mixing bowl, combine soup, mushrooms, water and Worcestershire sauce; blend well. Add soup mixture to rice mixture; mix well. Pour into greased 1½-quart casserole. Bake covered, at 375° for 30 minutes. Uncover; continue baking for 20 to 30 minutes until rice is done.

4 TO 6 SERVINGS

Tip: *Cream of celery, mushroom or golden mushroom soup can be used.

Disguise your leftovers in this very tasty casserole. A basic dish that's great for family suppers. Try serving with peas and a fruity salad.

Approximately 45 min.

TURKEY NOODLE BAKE

 1¼ cups (10½-oz. can) condensed cream
    of chicken soup
 ¼ cup water
 2 cups chopped turkey
 1 cup (2 stalks) chopped celery
 ½ cup coarsely chopped cashews,
    if desired
 1 tablespoon instant minced onion or
 ¼ cup chopped onion
 1 tablespoon chopped pimiento or green
    pepper
 2 cups (3-oz. can) chow mein noodles

Preheat oven to 350°. In greased 1½-quart casserole, combine soup and water. Stir to blend. Add diced turkey, celery, cashews, onion, pimiento and 1 cup of the noodles; mix well. Sprinkle remaining 1 cup noodles on top. Bake, uncovered, at 350° for 30 to 40 minutes until hot and bubbly.   4 SERVINGS

Approximately 55 min.

CHICKEN A LA SPECIAL

 2½ to 3 lbs. frying chicken, cut-up
 2 tablespoons butter or margarine
 ½ teaspoon salt
 ⅛ teaspoon pepper
 1¼ cups (10½-oz. can) condensed cream
    of mushroom soup
 ¾ cup dairy or imitation sour cream
 ½ cup (5-oz. can) deviled ham
 ½ cup (half 4-oz. pkg.) shredded Cheddar
    cheese

In large fry pan, brown chicken in butter; add salt, pepper and mushroom soup. Reduce heat; simmer, covered, for 30 to 40 minutes, until chicken is tender. Add remaining ingredients; stir gently into sauce. Continue heating until cheese is melted. (Do not boil; sour cream will separate.) If desired, top with toasted buttered bread crumbs to serve. Serve hot.
          4 TO 6 SERVINGS

Turkey Divan
Confetti Cheese Bread, page 109
Pineapple and Cottage Cheese
Beverage
Apple Cinnamon Upside Down Cake,
page 120
MENU PREPARATION TIME: 1 HR.

SUGGESTED ALTERNATES

Bread: A dish with some spunky color — maybe Rice Jardiniere, page 106 or Cheesy Barbecue Rolls, page 109.

Salad: Make it refreshing and slightly tangy, such as a fruit combination.

Dessert: A chewy and sweet something, such as Almond Bear Claws, page 118, or Banana Boats, page 121.

TIME HELPS: The main dish takes the longest time to fix, so start that first. Then, assemble the Confetti Cheese Bread and place it in the oven to bake with the Turkey Divan. Prepare the dessert and place it also in the oven.

While those are baking, assemble the salad on individual serving dishes. Then, when everything is ready, serve it hot.

Approximately 1 hr.

TURKEY DIVAN

 3 cups (two 10-oz. pkgs.) frozen broccoli
    spears or pieces
 6 thick slices turkey
 1¼ cups (10½-oz. can) condensed cream
    of chicken soup
 ¼ cup mayonnaise or salad dressing
 1 teaspoon lemon juice
 ½ cup prepared toasted bread crumbs
 1 tablespoon melted butter or margarine

Preheat oven to 375°. Cook broccoli as directed on package; drain. Arrange broccoli in bottom of greased 9-inch baking dish. Lay turkey slices on top. In small mixing bowl, combine soup, mayonnaise and lemon juice. Pour over turkey slices. Combine bread crumbs and butter; sprinkle on top. Bake, uncovered, at 375° for 20 to 30 minutes until heated.   4 SERVINGS

Turkey Divan Menu

Pork and Ham

Start with chow mein meat or equal parts of pork and veal cut into small, thin strips. Serve with a fruity salad.

Approximately 45 min.
CHOW MEIN

- 1 lb. chow mein meat
- 1 tablespoon oil or shortening
- 1 cup (8 oz. or ½ pt.) sliced fresh mushrooms
- 1 medium onion, sliced
- 1 cup (2 stalks) sliced celery
- ½ teaspoon salt
- ½ teaspoon ground ginger
- 3 tablespoons soy sauce
- 1 bouillon cube or 1 teaspoon instant bouillon
- 1 cup water
- 2 cups (1-lb. can) drained bean sprouts
- ½ cup (5-oz. can) drained, sliced water chestnuts
- ½ cup (5-oz. can) drained bamboo shoots
- 1 tablespoon cornstarch
- 2 tablespoons water

In fry pan, brown meat in hot oil. Add mushrooms and onion; brown slightly. Add celery, salt, ginger, soy sauce, bouillon and 1 cup water. Cover and simmer 20 minutes. Add bean sprouts, water chestnuts and bamboo shoots. Combine cornstarch with 2 tablespoons water. Stir into meat mixture; bring to boil, stirring constantly. Cover and simmer 15 more minutes. Serve over chow mein noodles or rice.   4 SERVINGS

> Tips: Two cups (1-lb. can) drained chow mein vegetables can be used for bean sprouts, water chestnuts and bamboo shoots.
>
> For crisper vegetables, add onion and celery along with bean sprouts.
>
> If desired, use 1 package (⅝ oz.) Pillsbury Brown Gravy Mix for salt, bouillon cube and cornstarch.

Approximately 40 min.
APRICOT GLAZED PORK CHOPS

- 4 pork rib or loin chops, ½ inch thick
- 1 teaspoon salt
- 1 tablespoon oil or shortening
- 1⅓ cups (1-lb. can) apricot halves, drain and reserve liquid
- Reserved apricot liquid plus water to make 1½ cups
- 2 tablespoons cornstarch
- 2 teaspoons lemon juice
- 2 tablespoons slivered almonds

Sprinkle chops with salt. Brown in oil on both sides in fry pan. Add ½ cup of the apricot liquid. Cover; reduce heat and simmer for 10 minutes. Combine cornstarch and remaining 1 cup apricot liquid; add to chops. Continue simmering, stirring frequently, until liquid thickens. Add apricots and almonds. Cover; continue simmering 10 minutes. Serve.
          4 SERVINGS

A basic, favorite recipe. Try serving it with spinach, warm rolls and coleslaw.

Approximately 1 hr.
BREADED PORK CHOPS

- 6 rib or loin pork chops, cut ¾ to 1-inch thick
- ½ cup dry bread crumbs or cracker crumbs
- 1 teaspoon salt
- ¼ teaspoon pepper
- 1 egg, slightly beaten
- 3 tablespoons oil or shortening
- ⅓ cup water
- ½ teaspoon Worcestershire sauce

In shallow dish or bowl, combine bread crumbs, salt and pepper. Dip pork chops into egg, then into bread crumb mixture. Brown chops in hot oil on both sides in large fry pan. Add water and Worcestershire sauce. Cover and simmer 35 to 50 minutes, until tender. Uncover and continue cooking about 10 minutes until coating is crisp.   6 SERVINGS

Easily done inside with prepared barbecue sauce. Corn, beans and coleslaw make tasty side-dishes.

Approximately 45 min.

SKILLET BARBECUED PORK CHOPS

1 tablespoon oil or shortening

4 to 6 pork rib or loin chops, cut ¾ to 1-inch thick

½ teaspoon salt

⅓ to ½ cup prepared barbecue sauce

1 lemon, sliced

Brown chops in oil in large fry pan, drain excess fat. Sprinkle with salt. Top with barbecue sauce. Simmer, covered, for 25 to 30 minutes until chops are tender. Place lemon slices on top of chops and simmer, uncovered, 5 minutes. 4 TO 6 SERVINGS

A great dish for guests. Sweet potatoes, a green vegetable and a marinated salad would top off a colorful and tasty meal.

Approximately 50 min.

BREADED PORK TENDERLOIN IN WINE SAUCE

1 lb. pork tenderloin, cut into ¾ to 1-inch thick pieces

¼ cup flour

2 tablespoons grated Parmesan cheese

¼ teaspoon salt

⅛ teaspoon pepper

2 to 3 tablespoons butter or margarine

½ tablespoon cornstarch

½ cup cold water

2 teaspoons beef flavored instant bouillon or 2 bouillon cubes

¼ cup sherry

Flatten each piece of tenderloin with meat hammer into patties. Combine flour, cheese, salt and pepper. Dip meat patties into flour mixture to coat well. In large fry pan, brown meat in butter on both sides. Cover and cook over very low heat for 25 to 30 minutes until tender. Remove to heated platter. Combine cornstarch with water. Add bouillon and sherry; mix well. Stir cornstarch mixture into pan drippings. Cook over low heat until thickened and smooth. Pour over meat to serve.

4 SERVINGS

A quick and economical dish that would be great with sweet-sour vegetables.

Approximately 30 min.

PORK FRIED RICE

1 package (4 oz.) fried rice mix

½ lb. (2) pork steaks, cut into ½-inch cubes*

1 tablespoon oil or shortening

1 egg, slightly beaten

2 tablespoons chopped green pepper, if desired

Prepare rice mix as directed on package, except for frying. Meanwhile brown meat in hot oil in large fry pan; add egg and continue browning until egg is cooked. Add rice and green pepper; continue frying as directed on package. To serve, top with parsley sprigs or sliced green onion. 3 TO 4 SERVINGS

Tip: *Scissors offer convenience for cutting meat into cubes.

Pineapple liquid adds a unique tang to prepared barbecue sauce mix. Broil or grill the chops and pineapple together for a taste delight. Complete your meal with squash, a marinated vegetable salad and hot rolls.

Approximately 30 min.

SASSY BARBECUED PORK 'N PINEAPPLE

1¼ cups (1 lb. 4-oz. can) pineapple rings, drain and reserve ⅔ cup liquid

1 package (¾ oz.) barbecue sauce mix*

Reserved ⅔ cup pineapple liquid

1 cup (8-oz. can) tomato sauce

6 or 8 rib or loin pork chops, about 1½-inches thick

Salt

Pepper

Preheat broiler. In small saucepan, combine barbecue sauce mix, pineapple liquid and tomato sauce. Cook over medium low heat, stirring occasionally, until mixture thickens and comes to a boil. Broil or grill pork chops 3 to 4 inches from heat, brushing occasionally with sauce for 8 to 10 minutes on each side. Place pineapple rings on broiler pan or grill during last 5 minutes; broil or grill, brushing occasionally with sauce. Sprinkle chops with salt and pepper; serve with glazed pineapple rings. 6 TO 8 SERVINGS

Mushroom Braised Pork Steaks Menu

Mushroom Braised Pork Steaks
Speedy Baked Potatoes, page 105
Pimiento Cheese Peas, page 101
Wilted Lettuce Salad, page 88
Beverage
Cinnamon Apple Bake, page 114
MENU PREPARATION TIME: 1 HR.

Cater to your particular budget by using either steaks, chops or tenderloin in this dish that's flavored with mushroom soup. Very easy, as well as quick. Family and guests will like this one.

SUGGESTED ALTERNATES

Potatoes: Another mild-flavored potato dish or something like Noodles Alfredo, page 106, or Crunchy Onion Mini-Loaves, page 108.

Vegetable: Make it colorful and flavorful — for example, Sherried Carrots, page 99, Dilly Green Beans, page 95, or buttered corn.

Salad: A combination of greens, vegetables and/or fruits with a tangy dressing.

Desserts: Apple and other fruit flavors are great. Try chilled applesauce, Applemallow Bake, page 116, or Pineapple Cream Pie, page 123.

TIME HELPS: The pork steaks require the longest cooking time, so start them first. As soon as the main dish is simmering, place the potatoes in the oven for baking.

About 40 minutes before dinner time, begin baking the apples. (When dinner is ready, turn the oven off and open the door slightly. The apples will stay warm until dessert time.)

Prepare the greens for the salad; then cook the peas. Final additions to the salad and peas can be made just before serving.

Approximately 1 hr.
MUSHROOM BRAISED PORK STEAKS

- 6 pork steaks (about 1½ lbs.)
- 1 teaspoon salt
- ¼ teaspoon garlic powder
- ¼ teaspoon pepper
- 1¼ cups (10½ oz.) golden mushroom soup
- ⅔ cup (4 oz.) undrained mushroom stems and pieces

In large fry pan, brown pork steaks on both sides. Sprinkle with salt, garlic powder and pepper. Stir mushroom soup and mushrooms into meat. Reduce heat. Simmer, covered, over low heat, 45 to 50 minutes, until tender.

4 TO 6 SERVINGS

Tip: Pork chops or pork tenderloin can be used for the pork steaks. Simmering time for the chops will be 35 to 40 minutes; for tenderloin slices about ¾-inch thick, 20 to 30 minutes.

Sweet-Sour Pork
Fluffy Rice
Buttered Asparagus
Strawberry Gelatin Salad, (see Tip,
Spicy Peach Salad, page 90)
Tea
Quick Coconut Delights, page 117
MENU PREPARATION TIME: 1 HR.

SUGGESTED ALTERNATES

Vegetable: A green vegetable with a mild flavor — buttered snow pea pods, Onion Simmered Beans, page 97, or a plain or buttered vegetable.

Salad: Fruit Slaw, page 91, Spicy Peach Salad, page 90, or any fruity combination.

Dessert: Something chewy with an almond or coconut flavor, such as Almond Bear Claws, page 118.

TIME HELPS: Prepare the salad first (see Tip on Spicy Peach Salad, page 104) so that it can chill as long as possible; then prepare and start baking the dessert. (It should cool slightly during dinner and be just right by dessert time.) The main dish falls into the time line next so it can simmer for tenderness.

Start the rice either before the asparagus — if you're using regular rice — or after it if you're using quick-cooking rice.

Serve this meal with chopsticks or silverware for a great meal with an Oriental flair.

A flavorful dish for a quick dinner. Serve it family style, or serve it with an Oriental theme for guests. Very attractive and tasty.

Approximately 30 min.

SWEET-SOUR PORK

- 1 lb. lean boneless pork, cut into 1-inch cubes
- 2 tablespoons oil or shortening
- ½ teaspoon salt
- ¾ cup water
- 1½ cups (13½-oz. can) pineapple chunks, drain and reserve ½ cup pineapple liquid
- ¼ cup sugar
- 2 tablespoons cornstarch
- ½ cup pineapple liquid reserved
- 3 to 4 tablespoons vinegar
- 1 tablespoon soy sauce
- ½ cup green pepper pieces

In large fry pan, brown pork cubes on all sides in oil. Season with salt. Reduce heat; add ¾ cup water. Simmer, covered, 20 to 30 minutes until pork is tender. In small mixing bowl, combine sugar, cornstarch, vinegar, pineapple liquid and soy sauce. Add sauce to meat in fry pan; cook, stirring constantly, until clear and thickened. Add green pepper pieces and drained pineapple. Continue cooking, covered, over low heat 5 to 10 minutes until green pepper is crisp-tender. Serve over hot fluffy rice.   4 SERVINGS

Pictured on page 12

Approximately 50 min.

BRAISED PORK CHOPS

- 6 rib, loin or shoulder pork chops, cut ¾ to 1-inch thick
- ½ teaspoon salt
- ⅛ teaspoon pepper
- ¼ cup water, fruit juice or vegetable juice

Brown chops on both sides in large fry pan. Season with salt and pepper; add water. Cover; simmer 45 to 60 minutes until tender.
6 SERVINGS

A quick sauce gives a super flavor. Heat extra sauce until thickened and serve over potatoes or rice. Add some zucchini or summer squash and a salad for a great meal.

Approximately 50 min.

SPEEDY MARINATED PORK CHOPS

- ½ cup catsup
- ½ cup water
- 1 teaspoon Worcestershire sauce
- 1 package (⅝ oz.) Pillsbury Home Style Gravy Mix
- 4 rib or loin pork chops, cut ¾ to 1-inch thick

Preheat broiler. Combine all ingredients except pork chops in shallow pan. Add chops. Let stand ½ hour. Broil 3 to 4 inches from heat or grill over hot coals 8 to 10 minutes on each side, brushing frequently with sauce. Serve with sauce or serve sauce with potatoes or rice.
4 SERVINGS

Leftovers star in this speedy dish. Complete the meal with a beet salad and green vegetable.

Approximately 15 min.

DEVILED HAM ON NOODLES

- 1 package (⅝ oz.) Pillsbury Home Style Gravy Mix
- 2 teaspoons sugar
- 1 tablespoon prepared mustard
- 2 cups cubed ham or luncheon meat
- 4 servings cooked noodles

Prepare gravy mix as directed on package, adding sugar and dry mustard before cooking. Add ham or luncheon meat and heat thoroughly. Serve hot over noodles. 4 SERVINGS

This attractive and flavorful dish is especially well-suited to light suppers or lunches. Prepared foods shortcut your time.

Approximately 45 min.

HAM ASPARAGUS HOLLANDAISE

- 1 package (10 oz.) frozen asparagus spears or pieces*
- 3 tablespoons (half of 3-oz. pkg.) cream cheese
- ¼ cup mayonnaise or salad dressing
- ½ lb. (two 4-oz. pkgs.) thinly sliced ham
- 1 package (1⅝ oz.) hollandaise sauce mix or ⅔ cup prepared hollandaise sauce
- 1 hard cooked egg, sliced or chopped

Preheat oven to 350°. Cook asparagus as directed on package; drain water when tender. Meanwhile, soften cream cheese in small mixing bowl; add mayonnaise and blend thoroughly. Spread cream cheese mixture on ham slices. Roll one or two asparagus spears inside each ham slice. Secure with toothpicks. Place in 13x9-inch baking dish. Prepare hollandaise sauce mix as directed on package. Pour thickened sauce over ham rolls. Bake, uncovered, at 350° for 10 to 15 minutes until heated through. Garnish with egg. Serve at once.
4 TO 5 SERVINGS

This hearty dish can be a great disguise for leftover ham. A sliced tomato salad and buttered broccoli would make nice meal mates.

Approximately 1 hr.

SCALLOPED POTATOES AND HAM

- 1 package (7¼ oz.) Pillsbury Scalloped Potato Mix
- 2 to 3 cups ham cubes
- ¾ cup (half of 10-oz. pkg.) frozen peas
- 1 teaspoon instant minced onion
- 1 teaspoon Worcestershire sauce
- 2¼ cups water
- ¾ cup milk
- ¼ cup toasted bread crumbs, if desired

Preheat oven to 350°. Combine potato mix with seasoning packet, ham, frozen peas, onion and Worcestershire sauce, in ungreased 1½-quart casserole. Pour water and milk over all; mix well. Sprinkle toasted bread crumbs on top. Bake, uncovered, at 350° for 45 to 50 minutes until potatoes are tender.
4 SERVINGS

*Try Polynesian flavors for a barbecue. Good
accompanying dishes might include rice, green
beans and a cottage cheese salad.*

Approximately 25 min.
SWEET 'N SOUR HAM STEAK
- 1½ cups (13½-oz. can) pineapple chunks,
  drain and reserve ⅓ cup liquid
- Reserved ⅓ cup pineapple liquid
- ⅓ cup vinegar
- ⅓ cup water
- ⅓ cup firmly packed brown sugar
- 1 package (⅝ oz.) Pillsbury Home Style
  Gravy Mix
- 2 smoked ham slices, cut ½ inch thick

Preheat broiler. Combine reserved pineapple
liquid, vinegar, water, sugar and gravy mix in
small saucepan. Blend well; heat just to boiling
point. Place ham on rack 3 to 4 inches from
broiler or above hot coals. Grill 10 minutes;
brush with sauce. Turn, brush with sauce and
grill 10 minutes longer. Heat pineapple chunks
with remaining sauce just before serving. Spoon
over ham slices to serve. 4 TO 6 SERVINGS

*Flavored gelatin provides the convenience clue
to this dish. Peach and ham flavors combine for
a real treat from your broiler or grill. Very good
with potato salad, broccoli and a fruit salad.*

Approximately 35 min.
PEACHY GRILLED HAM SLICE
- 1 package (3 oz.) peach-flavored gelatin
- ¼ cup firmly packed brown sugar
- ½ cup water
- 2 tablespoons lemon juice
- 1½ to 2 lbs. center cut ham slice, cut 1 to
  1½-inches thick

Preheat broiler. In small saucepan, combine
brown sugar, gelatin, water and lemon juice.
Heat, stirring constantly, over medium heat until
gelatin and sugar are dissolved. Broil or grill
ham slice 4 to 6 inches from heat for 15 minutes
on each side, basting occasionally with glaze.
If desired, place peach halves beside ham slice
during last 10 minutes of broiling or grilling,
basting occasionally with glaze. Serve ham
slice with remaining glaze and peach halves,
if desired. 6 TO 8 SERVINGS

*Colorful and sweet, this dish turns into a fine
meal with a green vegetable (spinach or
broccoli are really good) and a quick gelatin
salad.*

Approximately 1 hr.
HAM SLICE WITH SWEET POTATOES AND PINEAPPLE
- 2 lb. center cut ham slice, about 1-inch
  thick
- 1½ cups (12-oz. pkg.) frozen sweet potatoes
- 1½ cups (13¼-oz. can) undrained
  pineapple chunks
- ¼ cup orange juice concentrate, undiluted
- ¼ cup water
- ¼ cup firmly packed brown sugar
- 2 tablespoons cornstarch
- ¼ teaspoon cinnamon, if desired

Preheat oven to 350°. Cut ham into serving
pieces. Place in bottom of ungreased 1½-quart
casserole. Arrange frozen sweet potatoes
around ham. In small saucepan, combine
pineapple chunks, juice concentrate, water,
brown sugar, cornstarch and cinnamon; mix
well. Cook over low heat, stirring constantly,
until mixture thickens and comes to a boil.
Spoon sauce over ham and sweet potatoes.
Bake, uncovered, at 350° for 40 to 50 minutes
until sweet potatoes are tender.
4 TO 6 SERVINGS

*The traditional pork and apple combination
takes a new twist with these ham kabobs.
Squash and a macaroni salad would be
interesting with this.*

Approximately 25 min.
FRUIT 'N HAM KABOBS
- ¾ cup (6-oz. can) frozen orange juice
  concentrate, thawed
- ¼ cup honey or firmly packed brown sugar
- 1½ lbs. ham, cut into 1-inch cubes
- 3 apples, cored and cut into eighths

Preheat broiler. In small bowl or measuring cup,
combine orange juice concentrate and honey;
mix well. Thread ham and apple pieces
alternately on skewer. Broil or grill 3 to 4 inches
from heat, brushing occasionally with orange
mixture, for 5 to 7 minutes on each side until
cooked through and lightly browned. Serve
with additional orange mixture, if desired.
6 KABOBS

Port Glazed Ham
Tropical Tater Broil, page 105
Buttered Peas
Basic Sour Cream Coleslaw, page 87
Beverage
Pineapple Cream Pie, page 123
MENU PREPARATION TIME: 1 HR.

SUGGESTED ALTERNATES

Vegetables: A sweet potato or squash dish — such as Maple Glazed Sweets, page 104, or Squash Vermont, page 102 — and a mild flavored green vegetable — such as Onion Simmered Beans, page 97, or Bacon Fried Beans, page 97.

Salad: A coleslaw variation or a fruit and vegetable combination, such as Carrot-Raisin Salad, page 89.

Dessert: Apple or other fruit flavors are nice — for instance, Cinnamon Apple Bake, page 114, or Saucy Apple Swirl Cake, page 120.

TIME HELPS: Prepare the dessert first, then combine the ingredients for the ham glaze and begin broiling the ham on the first side. In between occasional bastings, prepare the coleslaw and place it in the refrigerator to chill.

After turning ham to broil second side, start cooking peas and assemble Tropical Tater Broil. During last 5 minutes of broiling, place Tropical Tater Broil under broiler beside ham.

Add the remaining ingredients for the peas, then you're ready to serve.

Super easy and extra good. Family and guests alike will enjoy this dish. Make the meal casual or fancy by the side dishes you choose.

Approximately 40 min.

PORT GLAZED HAM
   ½ **cup Port wine or fruit juice**
   ¼ **cup firmly packed brown sugar or honey**
   1 **smoked ham slice, cut 1½-inches thick**

Combine wine and brown sugar in measuring cup. Place ham slice on rack in broiler pan. Broil or grill 4 to 5 inches from heat for 15 to 20 minutes on each side, basting frequently with wine mixture.   4 TO 6 SERVINGS

*Port Glazed
Ham Grill Menu*

Veal and Lamb

The mild flavor of chicken gravy provides a fine flavor addition to veal. Serve it with cauliflower, a green vegetable and a fruity salad.

Approximately 35 min.
ZESTY VEAL CHOPS
  ¼ cup flour
  6 veal chops (about 1½ lb.)
  1 teaspoon salt
  ½ teaspoon leaf oregano
  Dash pepper
  2 tablespoons butter or margarine
  1¼ cups (10¼-oz. can) chicken gravy
  ¼ to ½ cup water

In plastic or paper bag, shake chops in flour. Brown chops on both sides in butter in large fry pan, sprinkling with salt, oregano and pepper during browning. Add chicken gravy and water. Reduce heat; simmer, covered, for 20 to 30 minutes until meat is tender. (If sauce becomes too thick, add small amount of water.) Serve with sauce.   6 SERVINGS

Add leftover veal to spaghetti sauce for a new and different main dish. Add tossed salad and hot French bread for a sure success.

Approximately 35 min.
SPAGHETTI SAUCE DE VEAUX
  2 to 3 cups cubed cooked veal
  2 packages (1 oz. each) Pillsbury
    Spaghetti Sauce Mix
  1¼ cups water
  2 cups (1-lb. can) undrained tomatoes
  ¾ cup (6-oz. can) tomato paste

In large saucepan, combine all ingredients. Bring to a boil over medium heat. Reduce heat; simmer, covered, ½ hour. Serve hot over spaghetti or noodles. 6 TO 8 SERVINGS SAUCE

Simple flavors make great harmony together in this recipe. Broiled tomatoes and a salad of greens would complete the menu nicely.

Approximately 40 min.
BROWN 'N HEARTY VEAL CHOPS
  4 veal chops (about 1 lb.)
  3 tablespoons butter or margarine
  ¼ cup chopped green onion, if desired
  ½ cup water
  1 package (7 oz.) beef flavored rice mix
  1½ cups boiling water

In large fry pan, brown veal in butter on both sides. Add onion and ½ cup water. Reduce heat. Simmer, covered, 20 to 30 minutes until meat is tender. Remove chops from pan. Place rice mix in pan with drippings. Add boiling water. Place chops on top of rice; continue simmering, covered, for 10 to 15 minutes until water is absorbed.   4 SERVINGS

A pineapple sauce with almonds offers a quick way to dress up leftover veal. Try serving with cooked carrots and a wedge of lettuce.

Approximately 20 min.
VEAL ALMOND
  2 tablespoons butter or margarine
  2 chicken bouillon cubes or 2 teaspoons
    instant bouillon
  2 cups water
  2 tablespoons cornstarch
  1 cup (8¼-oz. can) undrained crushed
    pineapple
  2 to 3 cups cubed cooked veal
  ½ cup toasted slivered almonds
  ½ cup (1 stalk) sliced celery
  1 teaspoon salt

Melt butter in fry pan. Add bouillon and water; bring to a boil and reduce heat. Blend cornstarch and pineapple; add gradually to liquid, stirring constantly, until mixture boils and thickens. Add veal, almonds, celery and salt. Bring to boil and simmer 5 to 10 minutes. Serve over chow mein noodles or rice. 6 SERVINGS

Parmesan cheese is a delicious accent to veal. These breaded cutlets are easy and great for company. A vinaigrette salad and green vegetable would go well with this dish.

Approximately 30 min.

VEAL PARMESAN

½ cup grated Parmesan cheese
¼ cup dry bread or cracker crumbs
½ teaspoon paprika
¼ teaspoon salt
⅛ teaspoon pepper
4 veal cutlets
1 egg, slightly beaten
2 to 3 tablespoons oil or shortening
4 slices or 1 cup shredded Mozzarella cheese, if desired
½ cup canned or 4 slices fresh tomato, if desired

Combine Parmesan cheese, bread crumbs, paprika, salt and pepper. Dip veal into egg, then into crumb mixture. In fry pan, heat oil; fry cutlets until golden brown on one side; turn. If desired, top browned side with Mozzarella cheese and tomato section. Reduce heat and continue cooking until veal is done and cheese has melted, about 10 minutes. 4 SERVINGS

Elegance is the word for these subtly flavored veal chops — both in color and in appearance. They'd be terrific for guests; serve them with asparagus, glazed carrots and a marinated salad.

Approximately 35 min.

VEAL CHOPS PERU

½ cup flour
5 to 6 veal chops (about 1½ lb.)
1 teaspoon salt
1 teaspoon leaf oregano
2 tablespoons butter or margarine
¼ cup water
1 onion, sliced
½ cup dairy or imitation sour cream
⅛ teaspoon instant coffee

In plastic or paper bag, shake chops in flour. In large fry pan, brown chops well on both sides in butter, sprinkling with salt and oregano during browning. Reduce heat; add water and onion. Cover; simmer 20 minutes until chops are tender. Remove chops to heated platter. Add sour cream and instant coffee to pan drippings; stir to combine. Pour sauce over chops. If desired, garnish with parsley.

5 TO 6 SERVINGS

Tip: Lamb chops can be used for the veal chops. Prepare as directed.

Elegant and delicious. Some good side dishes might be noodles, a flavored green vegetable and a fruity salad.

Approximately 30 min.

VEAL SCALLOPINI

1½ lbs. veal round steak, cut ¼-inch thick
¼ cup flour
1 teaspoon salt
⅛ teaspoon pepper
2 tablespoons butter or margarine
1 cup (8 oz. or ½ pt.) sliced fresh or canned mushrooms
¼ cup dry sherry or white wine
¼ cup water
1 to 2 tablespoons chopped chives
1 tablespoon lemon juice
¼ teaspoon leaf rosemary, tarragon or marjoram

Cut steak into 4 to 6 serving pieces. Combine flour, salt and pepper; coat meat with seasoned flour. Pound meat with meat hammer or the edge of heavy saucer until ¼-inch thick, sprinkling with flour mixture as needed. In a large fry pan, brown both sides of veal in hot butter until golden brown. Add mushrooms, sherry, water, chives, lemon juice and rosemary. Simmer, covered, for 10 minutes. Remove meat to platter and spoon sauce over meat.   4 TO 6 SERVINGS

Tips: If desired, omit sherry and increase water to ½ cup.

Simple Saucy Veal Chops
Mashed Potatoes
Cheesy Fried Zucchini, page 102
Carrot-Raisin Salad, page 89
Beverage
Baked Fruit Ambrosia, page 113
MENU PREPARATION TIME: 50 MIN.

SUGGESTED ALTERNATES

Potatoes: Instant or regular mashed potatoes or a mashed potato variation or casserole.

Vegetable: Something green with a slight flavor twist — Skillet Fried Okra, page 101, or Dilly Green Beans, page 95.

Salad: A colorful and slightly tangy salad, such as Bean O' Relish Salad, page 88, Carrot Orange Toss, page 90, or a vegetable and lettuce combination.

Dessert: End the meal with a fruit-flavored dessert — Sherry Broiled Grapefruit, page 114, Cherry Crisp, page 121, or Banana Boats, page 121.

TIME HELPS: Start the dessert first and place it in the oven for baking. Next, brown the chops and begin simmering them. While they're cooking, prepare the salad and chill until serving time.

Then, fix the zucchini. (If waiting is necessary, the squash can be kept warm in the oven.) The instant mashed potatoes are last. (If you prefer regular mashed potatoes, start them before the squash.)

When the veal chops are tender, serve the main course and allow the dessert to cool slightly so that it will be a nice temperature for eating by dessert-time.

Gravy mix, mushrooms and water chestnuts give a simply grand flourish to the mild flavor of veal chops. Very attractive and tasty enough for guests.

Approximately 40 min.
SIMPLE SAUCY VEAL CHOPS

> 4 to 6 veal chops
> ¼ cup dry bread crumbs or flour
> 1 teaspoon salt
> 2 tablespoons butter or margarine
> 1 cup water
> 1 package (⅝ oz.) Pillsbury Brown Gravy Mix
> ½ cup (5-oz. can) drained and sliced water chestnuts
> 1 cup (½ pt. or 8 oz.) fresh mushrooms or ½ cup (4-oz. can) drained mushrooms

Coat chops with bread crumbs; sprinkle with salt. In large fry pan, brown chops in butter until deep brown (thorough browning makes flavor richer). Add ½ cup of the water; cover. Reduce heat; simmer 10 minutes. Combine gravy mix and remaining ½ cup water in measuring cup. Add gravy mixture, mushrooms and water chestnuts to chops. Continue simmering, covered, for 10 to 15 minutes, until meat is tender. Serve with gravy.

4 TO 6 SERVINGS

Simple Saucy Veal Chops Menu

Far Eastern flavors are combined here. The rice mix makes preparation easier for you and requires fewer ingredients. Try serving this with artichokes and carrots.

Approximately 50 min.
LAMB AND RICE SAFFRON

    5 to 6 (1½ to 2 lbs.) lamb shoulder steaks
        or chops
    1 tablespoon butter or margarine
    ½ cup water
    1 onion, sliced
    ½ teaspoon salt
    1 package (6 oz.) saffron or curried rice
        mix
    1½ cups water
    2 tablespoons brown sugar
    1 beef bouillon cube or 1 teaspoon
        instant bouillon
    ½ cup dairy or imitation sour cream

In large fry pan, brown steaks in butter on both sides. Add water, onion and salt. Reduce heat; cover. Simmer 15 minutes. Push meat to one side; stir remaining ingredients except sour cream into pan drippings. Continue simmering, covered, 20 to 25 minutes until most of water is absorbed. Stir in sour cream; heat through. To serve lamb and rice mixture, garnish with parsley if desired.   5 TO 6 SERVINGS

Great for using leftover lamb or cubes cut from fresh lamb. Try serving it with a sweet vegetable and a crisp tossed salad.

Approximately 45 min.
QUICK LAMB CURRY

    1½ lbs. boneless lamb shoulder, cut into
        1-inch cubes
    1 tablespoon oil or shortening
    ½ teaspoon salt
    ⅛ teaspoon pepper
    1¼ cups (10½-oz. can) condensed cream
        of mushroom soup
    1⅓ cups milk
    2 teaspoons curry powder

Brown meat slowly on all sides in oil in fry pan. Drain off fat. Sprinkle with salt and pepper. Combine soup, milk and curry powder. Stir into fry pan. Cover and simmer for 30 minutes until meat is tender. Serve over cooked rice.
                                      6 SERVINGS

A mildly flavored sour cream sauce adds an elegant air to these lamb chops. Add cheese topped Brussels sprouts, potatoes and a sliced tomato salad for a tasty and attractive menu.

Approximately 35 min.
LAMB CHOPS DELUXE

    6 to 8 lamb chops
    1 tablespoon oil
    1 teaspoon salt
    Dash pepper
    1 medium onion, sliced
    ¼ cup water
    1 teaspoon caraway seeds or dill weed
    1 package (1½ oz.) sour cream sauce mix

In large fry pan, brown chops well in oil on both sides. Drain excess fat. Add salt, pepper, onion, water and caraway seeds. Cover; reduce heat. Simmer 20 to 25 minutes until cooked through. Meanwhile prepare sour cream sauce mix as directed on package. Remove chops from pan to heated platter. Add sour cream sauce to pan drippings; stir to blend well. Pour sauce over chops on platter. If desired, garnish with parsley sprigs before serving. 3 TO 4 SERVINGS

Fruit flavors and lamb go well together, especially with this easy sauce from prepared jelly. Fried eggplant, corn and a tossed salad could be side dishes for this one.

Approximately 30 min.
PLUM DELICIOUS LAMB

    4 to 6 (1½ to 2 lbs.) lamb shoulder steaks,
        cut into 1-inch cubes
    2 teaspoons butter or margarine
    1 teaspoon salt
    Dash pepper
    ½ cup plum jelly or preserves
    2 to 3 teaspoons lemon juice

In large fry pan, brown lamb cubes in butter Add remaining ingredients. Reduce heat. Simmer, covered, for 20 to 25 minutes until meat is tender and sauce is thickened slightly. Serve over rice.   4 SERVINGS

    Tip: Other flavors jelly or preserves can
    be used. Apricot, raspberry and ginger
    are other favorites of ours.

Orange Blossom Lamb
Quick Almond Currant Rice, page 107
Dilly Sweet Peas, page 101
Tossed Salad
Beverage
Minty Fruit Ice, page 119
MENU PREPARATION TIME: 30 MIN.

Delicately flavored lamb makes an interesting dish for special occasions. Choose accompanying dishes to make it a company or a family meal.

SUGGESTED ALTERNATES

Rice: Plain rice, a rice pilaf dish or Rice and Mushrooms, page 107, would go well.

Vegetable: A colorful one, such as Sherried Carrots, page 99, or Dilly Green Beans, page 95.

Dessert: Something refreshing and fruity — maybe Orange Rum Baked Bananas, page 113, or Mint Whip Peaches, page 115.

TIME HELPS: Start the lamb first so it can simmer to tenderness while you prepare the rice and peas. Make the salad last — just before serving.

Since the sherbet for Minty Fruit Ice must be kept frozen until the last minute, wait until you're ready to serve before assembling.

Approximately 30 min.
ORANGE BLOSSOM LAMB

    6 lamb chops
    2 tablespoons butter or margarine
    ¾ cup (6-oz. can) undiluted orange juice concentrate
    1 teaspoon salt
    Dash pepper
    1 to 2 onions, sliced
    1 to 2 teaspoons soy sauce, if desired

In large fry pan, brown chops in butter on both sides. Reduce heat; add remaining ingredients, stirring gently until orange juice concentrate has blended with pan juices. Simmer, covered, for 15 to 20 minutes, turning chops once during cooking, until meat is tender. Serve chops with sauce. If desired, garnish with orange slices.

4 TO 6 SERVINGS

Orange Blossom Lamb Menu

Sausages and Luncheon Meats

Great for supper, and kids will love it. Coleslaw and baked beans make nice meal mates.

Approximately 15 min.

BARBECUE FRANKS

　1 package (⅝ oz.) Pillsbury Home Style Gravy Mix
　1 cup water
　1 tablespoon instant minced onion or ¼ cup chopped onion
　1 cup catsup
　1 tablespoon prepared mustard
　10 wieners or frankfurters, cut into ½-inch slices

Prepare gravy mix as directed on package, adding onion before cooking. Stir in catsup and mustard. Add wiener slices. Cover; simmer for 10 minutes. Serve over warm buns.

6 TO 8 SERVINGS

Add your creativity to this dish by varying the meat used (see Tip). This flavorful and hearty dish would go well with a green vegetable and crisp salad.

Approximately 30 min.

SAUSAGE 'N BROWN RICE

　1 package (7 oz.) beef flavored rice mix
　1 ring bologna (12 oz. to 1 lb.), sliced*
　½ cup (5-oz. can) drained sliced water chestnuts
　2 tablespoons chopped green pepper

Prepare rice mix as directed on package. Remove skin from bologna and cut into ½-inch slices. Add bologna, water chestnuts and green pepper to prepare rice. Cover. Simmer over low heat 10 to 15 minutes until heated through. Serve with soy sauce, if desired. 4 SERVINGS

Tips: *Wieners, smokie links or canned luncheon meat can be used for the bologna. Prepare as directed.

If desired, ½ cup sliced celery can be used for the water chestnuts.

Very "old country" in flavor. Good meal accompaniments might include hard crunchy rolls and potato salad.

Approximately 40 min.

POLISH SAUSAGE AND SAUERKRAUT

　4 cups (1 lb. 12-oz. can or 1 qt.) sauerkraut
　1 medium apple, chopped
　¼ cup firmly packed brown sugar
　¼ cup water
　½ teaspoon caraway seed, if desired
　1 to 1½ lbs. Polish sausage or ring bologna

In saucepan, combine all ingredients except sausage; place sausage on top. Cover and simmer 30 minutes until heated through.

4 TO 6 SERVINGS

Tip: If desired, wieners or smokie links can be used for the Polish sausage.

A great snack or supper idea. Serve it hot with a tossed salad and your other favorite Italian accompaniments.

Approximately 40 min.

PEPPERONI PIZZA

　1 can (8 oz.) Pillsbury Refrigerated Quick Crescent Dinner Rolls
　1 cup (8-oz. can) tomato sauce
　1 teaspoon leaf oregano
　1 package (2 oz.) sliced pepperoni
　1 cup (4-oz. pkg.) shredded Mozzarella cheese

Preheat oven to 375°. Separate dough into 4 rectangles. Place on ungreased cookie sheet, overlapping edges slightly; press to form a 14x8-inch rectangle. Pinch edges to form a rim. Spread sauce evenly over dough; sprinkle with oregano. Arrange slices of pepperoni over sauce; sprinkle with cheese. Bake at 375° for 15 to 20 minutes until golden. Serve hot.　14x8-INCH PIZZA

A quick-to-fix family dish with a Mexican touch — chili, wieners and corn. Serve with extra chips and a salad.

Approximately 20 min.

QUICK MEXICAN WIENERS

    4 wieners, sliced diagonally ¼-inch thick

    2 cups (15-oz. can) chili with beans

    1 teaspoon prepared mustard

    ¼ cup catsup or chili sauce

    1 cup (4 oz.) shredded Cheddar cheese

    2 cups corn chips

In medium saucepan, combine all ingredients except corn chips and ¼ cup of cheese. Simmer 10 minutes. Stir in corn chips; immediately pour into serving dish and sprinkle with remaining cheese. Serve immediately.

                    4 TO 5 SERVINGS

A sweet-sour barbecue sauce gives a sensational flavor to these kabobs. Do them on the grill or in the broiler. Then make fun picnic fare with a potato or macaroni salad and a vegetable.

Approximately 20 min.

ISLAND FRANK KABOBS

    1 cup (13½-oz. can) pineapple chunks; drain and reserve ⅔ cup liquid

    Reserved ⅔ cup pineapple liquid

    1 package (¾ oz.) barbecue sauce mix

    1 cup (8-oz. can) tomato sauce

    1 lb. (10) wieners or frankfurters, cut into thirds*

    1 green pepper, cut into cubes

    10 sweet pickles, cut in half

Preheat broiler. In small saucepan, combine pineapple liquid, barbecue sauce mix and tomato sauce. Heat, stirring occasionally, until mixture comes to a boil. Thread wieners, pineapple, green pepper and pickle alternately on skewers. Broil or grill 2 to 3 inches from heat, brushing occasionally with sauce, for 3 to 4 minutes on each side until heated through and lightly browned.   10 KABOBS

    Tips: *Smokie links can be used for the wieners. Cook thoroughly.

    Prepared barbecue sauce can be used for the sauce mixture in recipe. Or, barbecue sauce mix can be prepared as directed on package, if desired.

Cabbage, cheese soup and bologna make this a quick and easy family supper. Good with a relish tray and rolls.

Approximately 30 min.

BOLOGNA AND CABBAGE SUPPER

    ½ to 1 medium head cabbage, shredded

    ¼ cup water

    ½ teaspoon salt

    1 ring (about 12 oz.) bologna

    1¼ cups (10¾-oz. can) condensed Cheddar cheese soup

    2 tablespoons prepared mustard

In large saucepan, cook cabbage with water and salt, covered, over medium heat until tender, about 10 minutes. Drain; top with bologna. Combine soup and mustard; spoon over bologna. Cover and simmer 15 to 20 minutes until bologna is heated through.

                    5 TO 6 SERVINGS

    Tip: This is also good with wieners in place of bologna.

Island Frank Kabobs

65

The fun flavors in this casserole take only a jiffy to assemble — great for family suppers. Additional corn chips and a salad complete the menu.

Approximately 45 min.

CHILI FRANK BEAN BAKE

    2 cups (15½-oz. can) drained kidney
        beans
    2 cups (15¾-oz. can) chili hot beans
    ½ cup (1 stalk) chopped celery
    2 tablespoons chopped green pepper
    6 to 9 frankfurters, cut into thirds
    1 cup (4 oz.) grated sharp Cheddar
        cheese or 1 cup crushed corn chips

Preheat oven to 350°. In ungreased casserole, combine all ingredients except grated cheese. Mix well. Sprinkle cheese or corn chips on top. Bake, uncovered, for 30 to 40 minutes until heated through and cheese is melted.   4 TO 6 SERVINGS

If your family likes liver, they'll love this served with mashed potatoes and a colorful salad or vegetable.

Approximately 45 min.

LIVER, BACON AND ONIONS

    1½ lbs. beef, veal, lamb or pork liver
    ¼ cup flour
    1 teaspoon salt
    ¼ teaspoon pepper
    6 slices bacon
    1½ cups (3 med.) sliced onions
    ½ cup water or red wine

Cut liver into serving pieces. Combine flour, salt and pepper. Coat liver with seasoned flour. Fry bacon in fry pan until crisp; remove bacon and keep warm. Sauté onion and liver in bacon drippings. Add water; cover and simmer 15 minutes for veal, lamb and pork liver; 30 minutes for beef liver. Serve, topped with the crisp bacon.   6 SERVINGS

These easy ingredients can be kept on hand for quick-as-a-wink creative cooking. Try serving this with potato salad, green beans and coleslaw.

Approximately 30 min.

BARBECUED LUNCHEON LOAF

    1 can (12 oz.) canned luncheon meat
    2 tablespoons catsup
    2 tablespoons orange marmalade
    1 teaspoon Worcestershire sauce
    ¼ teaspoon instant minced onion
    5 onion slices, if desired

Preheat oven to 325°. Slice luncheon meat into 6 slices. Arrange in shallow baking dish. Place one onion slice between each piece, if desired. In small mixing bowl, combine remaining ingredients. Spoon over meat. Bake, uncovered, 20 to 30 minutes, until heated through.
                      3 TO 4 SERVINGS

This recipe is a money saver, as well as a time saver. Add color and texture with peas and an orange and carrot salad.

Approximately 40 min.

CRUNCHY LUNCHEON LOAF

    4 serving recipe Pillsbury Hungry Jack
        Mashed Potatoes
    ½ cup creamed cottage cheese
    2 cups (3-oz. can) French fried onions,
        crushed
    1 can (12 oz.) luncheon meat

Preheat oven to 350°. Prepare 4 serving recipe mashed potatoes as directed on package. Blend in cottage cheese and ¾ can of crushed onion. Stand luncheon meat in shallow baking dish. Make 4 to 5 cuts down into loaf, about ¾ way through. Place spoonful of potatoes between each meat slice. Spoon remaining potatoes around meat. Sprinkle with remaining onions. Bake at 350° for 25 to 30 minutes.
                      3 TO 4 SERVINGS

Tip: If desired, place pineapple slices in cuts in meat. Spoon all potatoes in mounds around meat. Or, omit the onion rings and place thin slices of orange, cut in half, in the cuts along with some whole cloves. Bake as directed.

Use your choice of meat here for your own unique variation. Great and hearty fare for lunch or supper.

Approximately 45 min.
BOLOGNA AND GERMAN POTATO SALAD

1 package (7¼ oz.) Pillsbury Hash Brown Potato Mix

6 slices bacon

Reserved 2 tablespoons bacon drippings

1 tablespoon instant minced onion or ¼ cup chopped onion

½ teaspoon celery seed

1 egg, slightly beaten

¼ cup water

¼ cup vinegar

2 rings (12-oz. each) bologna

Cook potatoes as directed on package. Drain well. Meanwhile, in large fry pan, cook bacon until crisp. Remove and set aside. Reserve 2 tablespoons bacon drippings; sauté chopped onion in reserved bacon drippings until tender.

In small mixing bowl, combine beaten egg, water and vinegar. Add to cooked onion and stir constantly. Cook over low heat until thickened. Stir in drained potatoes and crumbled bacon. Arrange bologna on top. Cover and cook over low heat, 20 to 30 minutes, until heated through.   6 SERVINGS

This dish is easy to make and has great family appeal. It's easy on the budget, too.

Approximately 20 min.
APPLE-KRAUT WIENERS

1 lb. wieners, cut in half lengthwise

2 to 4 cups (one or two 1-lb. cans) sauerkraut

2 unpeeled apples, cut into chunks

¼ cup firmly packed brown sugar

In large saucepan, combine all ingredients. Heat over medium heat, stirring occasionally, about 15 minutes until heated through. Serve hot.   4 TO 6 SERVINGS

Apple Kraut Wieners

Fish and Seafood

Very basic; very easy! A creamy vegetable, a crisp salad and hot roll would go nicely with this dish. Lemon and other fruit flavored desserts make great finalés for fish dishes.

Approximately 20 min.
FISH STICKS ALMONDINE
- ½ lb. (8-oz. pkg.) frozen breaded fish sticks
- 3 tablespoons butter or margarine
- ¼ cup slivered almonds
- Few drops Tabasco sauce

In fry pan, fry frozen fish sticks in 2 tablespoons of the butter for 8 to 10 minutes until golden brown and heated through. Remove to heated serving dish. Brown almonds in remaining 1 tablespoon butter. Add Tabasco sauce to almonds; toss well. Sprinkle almonds over fish sticks. Garnish with parsley or orange slices.

4 SERVINGS

Tip: Frozen breaded fish fillets can be used for the fish sticks. Prepare as directed.

Make your side dishes while this one bakes. Something like a quick marinated salad, a leafy vegetable and hot rolls would fit this bill of fare.

Approximately 40 min.
SOUPER FISH STICKS
- 1 package (8 oz.) breaded fish sticks
- 1¼ cups (10-oz. can) frozen condensed cream of shrimp soup, thawed
- 1 teaspoon parsley flakes or chopped parsley
- 1 lemon, sliced

Preheat oven to 400°. Arrange fish in greased 1-quart baking dish or 8x8-inch dish. Spoon soup over sticks. Sprinkle with parsley. Top with lemon slices. Bake, uncovered, at 400° for 30 to 35 minutes until fish is heated through and flakes easily.

4 SERVINGS

Very easy to do, and fish goes lightly on the budget. Try serving with rice, beans and a gelatin salad.

Approximately 20 min.
FISH STICKS WITH CURRY SAUCE
- 1 package (8 oz.) fish sticks*
- 1 package (1½ oz.) sour cream sauce mix
- ½ teaspoon curry powder

Prepare fish sticks as directed on package. Prepare sauce mix as directed on package, adding curry powder. Serve curry sauce over fish sticks.

3 TO 4 SERVINGS

Tip: *Breaded fish fillets can be used for the fish sticks. Prepare as directed.

This dish is ready in a jiffy, so serve other quick dishes with it for added convenience. Tomato slices, buttered green beans or a Chinese cabbage salad could be some of your choices.

Approximately 15 min.
CREAMY TUNA CRUNCH
- ¾ cup (6½-oz. can) drained tuna
- 2 cups (16-oz. can) drained Chinese vegetables*
- 1¼ cups (10½-oz. can) condensed cream of mushroom soup
- ½ cup (5-oz. can) drained, sliced water chestnuts
- ¼ cup chopped green pepper, if desired
- 2½ cups (3-oz. can) chow mein noodles

In medium saucepan, combine tuna, Chinese vegetables, soup, water chestnuts and green pepper. Heat over medium heat for 5 to 10 minutes, stirring occasionally, until heated through. Serve hot over chow mein noodles.

4 SERVINGS

Tip: *Other vegetables or vegetable combinations can be used for the Chinese vegetables.

An interesting dish that's easy to do. Try serving with a crisp salad, crusty roll, and a little wine for an elegant dinner or supper.

Approximately 30 min.
SHRIMP CREOLE
1 package (12 oz.) frozen shrimp

2 tablespoons oil

1 tablespoon instant minced onion or ¼ cup chopped onion

¼ to ½ cup chopped green pepper

2 tablespoons cornstarch

½ teaspoon salt

½ teaspoon paprika

¼ teaspoon ground thyme

¼ teaspoon rosemary, if desired

⅛ teaspoon garlic powder

⅛ teaspoon pepper

3½ cups (1 lb. 12-oz. can) undrained tomatoes

Rinse frozen shrimp in cold water. Drain. In large fry pan, sauté chopped onion and green pepper in oil until tender. Add cornstarch, salt, paprika, thyme, rosemary, garlic powder and pepper. Blend well. Add tomatoes and shrimp. Simmer over low heat 15 to 20 minutes, stirring occasionally, until sauce is thickened and shrimp is cooked. Serve over hot fluffy rice or wild rice combination.   4 SERVINGS

Round out the flavors and color of this dish by serving accompaniments such as a tossed greens salad, buttered corn and hot rolls.

Approximately 40 min.
HALIBUT STEAKS IN TOMATO SAUCE
4 halibut steaks

Salt

Pepper

1 cup (8-oz. can) tomato sauce

2 tablespoons chopped green pepper

2 tablespoons chopped celery

½ teaspoon instant minced onion

½ teaspoon leaf oregano, if desired

¼ teaspoon leaf basil, if desired

Preheat oven to 350°. Wash and dry fish. Season with salt and pepper to taste. Place in greased baking dish. In small mixing bowl combine remaining ingredients; mix well. Spoon sauce over each piece of fish. Bake,

uncovered, at 350° for 25 to 30 minutes, or until fish flakes easily with a fork. To serve, garnish with parsley or lemon, if desired. 4 SERVINGS

Tip: The following fish steaks can be used for the halibut: haddock, swordfish, cod. Prepare as directed.

Flounder, sole, red snapper, pike or perch fillets can also be used; reduce baking time to 20 to 25 minutes.

A few herbs in the crumb topping for this dish add a speedy and flavorful touch to the fish. Broccoli and a fruity salad would be nice meal accompaniments for this.

Approximately 35 min.
BAKED SWORDFISH STEAK WITH HERB CRUMBS
1 large (1 lb.) swordfish steak

¼ cup butter or margarine, melted

Salt

Pepper

½ cup prepared toasted bread crumbs

1 teaspoon parsley flakes

½ teaspoon leaf tarragon*

¼ teaspoon celery seed, if desired

Preheat oven to 350°. Wash and dry fish. Place fish in greased baking dish. Brush with 2 tablespoons of the melted butter. Season with salt and pepper. In small mixing bowl, combine crumbs and seasonings. Add remaining 2 tablespoons melted butter and mix well. Spoon crumb mixture over fish. Bake at 350°, for 25 to 30 minutes, until fish flakes easily with a fork. Serve with lemon wedge.
                4 SERVINGS

Tips: *If desired, ½ teaspoon Italian seasoning can be used for the tarragon.

The following fish steaks can be used for the swordfish, halibut, haddock, cod. Prepare as directed.

Flounder, sole, perch, pike and red snapper fillets can also be used; reduce baking time to 20 to 25 minutes.

Broiled fish is simple and fast. Serve it plain or with one of the sauces. Colorful vegetables and crisp salads round out the texture and eye appeal of your meal.

Approximately 15 min.

BROILED FISH STEAKS OR FILLETS

4 fish steaks or 2 lbs. fish fillets

½ cup melted butter or margarine

Paprika

Salt

Pepper

Preheat broiler. Wash and dry fish. Arrange in single layer in greased broiler pan or shallow baking dish. Brush both sides with melted butter. Sprinkle with paprika, salt and pepper to taste. Place 2 inches from broiler. Broil whole fish or fish steaks 5 to 8 minutes on first side. Turn carefully. Broil second side until fish flakes easily with fork. (Second side takes less time.) Broil fish fillets only 3 to 5 minutes. To serve, garnish with lemon slices. 4 SERVINGS

> Tip: The following fish fillets or steaks can be used for broiling:
>
> | | |
> |---|---|
> | Cod | Halibut |
> | Red Snapper | Salmon |
> | Perch | Sole |
> | Pike | Swordfish |
> | Flounder | Bass |
> | Haddock | Trout |
>
> Broiling times will vary according to thickness.

Approximately 20 min.

SIMPLY GLAZED SALMON STEAKS

4 salmon steaks

Salt

Pepper

¼ cup butter or margarine, melted

¼ cup firmly packed brown sugar

2 to 3 tablespoons lemon juice

Preheat broiler. Place salmon steaks on broiler pan. Sprinkle with salt and pepper. In small bowl, combine remaining ingredients; mix well. Brush steaks with butter mixture. Broil 5 to 6 inches from heat, brushing occasionally, for 8 to 10 minutes on each side until fish flakes easily. (Second side will require less broiling time.) Serve with extra butter mixture or with lemon. 4 SERVINGS

Approximately 5 min.

QUICK CANTONESE SAUCE FOR SEAFOOD

2 tablespoons cooking oil

¼ cup chopped green pepper

1 teaspoon instant minced onion or
1 tablespoon chopped onion

½ cup prepared sweet-sour sauce

2 tablespoons soy or teriyaki sauce

In small fry pan, sauté green pepper and onion in oil until tender. Add sweet-sour and soy sauces. Simmer until heated through. Brush on lobster tails or other seafood while broiling or serve as a sauce with broiled or breaded shrimp. ¾ CUP SAUCE

Approximately 5 min.

ASPARAGUS SAUCE

1¼ cups (10½-oz. can) condensed cream of asparagus soup

2 tablespoons sherry or white wine

In small saucepan, combine soup and wine. Blend well. Simmer over low heat until heated through. 1⅓ CUPS SAUCE

Approximately 5 min.

CREAMY DILL SAUCE

1¼ cups (10½-oz. can) condensed cream of celery soup

2 tablespoons milk

¼ teaspoon dill weed

In small saucepan, combine all ingredients. Blend well. Simmer over low heat until heated through. 1¼ CUPS SAUCE

Approximately 5 min.

RAREBIT SAUCE

1¼ cups (10¾-oz. can) condensed Cheddar cheese soup

2 tablespoons milk

¼ cup chopped green chives

¼ teaspoon instant minced onion

2 tablespoons catsup

In small saucepan, combine soup and milk. Mix until well blended. Add remaining ingredients. Mix well. Simmer over low heat until heated through. 1½ CUPS SAUCE

> Tip: 1 package (2¼ oz.) cheese sauce mix can be used for the soup and milk. Prepare as directed on package.

Italian seasoning in a hollandaise sauce gives these salmon steaks an elegant appeal. Broccoli, parslied potatoes and a light salad would go well with this.

Approximately 15 min.

BROILED SALMON STEAKS WITH ZIPPY ITALIAN SAUCE

    4 salmon steaks, about ¾-inch thick
    ¼ cup butter or margarine, melted
    1 package (1⅝ oz.) hollandaise
      sauce mix
    ½ cup water
    ½ teaspoon Italian seasoning

Preheat broiler. Wash and dry fish. Brush broiler pan with melted butter. Place fish on broiler pan and brush with melted butter. Season with salt and pepper. Broil 5 to 6 inches from heat for 5 minutes. Turn; brush with melted butter. Continue broiling 5 more minutes. While fish broils, prepare sauce as directed on package, adding Italian seasoning mix. Remove fish carefully to hot platter and serve with sauce.   4 SERVINGS

   Tip: If desired, ¼ teaspoon each leaf oregano and leaf basil can be used for the Italian seasoning mix.

Approximately 15 min.

SAUCY SEAFOOD SUPREME

    2 to 2½ cups (two 7-oz. cans) drained
      seafood*
    1¼ cups (10½-oz. can) condensed cream
      of chicken soup**
    1 cup (2 stalks) chopped celery
    2 tablespoons chopped chives or
      1 tablespoon chopped green onion
    2 tablespoons butter or margarine
    ½ cup slivered almonds
    2 cups (3-oz. can) chow mein noodles

In medium saucepan, combine seafood, soup, celery and chives; mix well. Heat over medium heat, stirring occasionally, for 5 to 10 minutes, until heated through. Meanwhile, melt butter in small fry pan. Brown almonds in butter; remove from heat. Place chow mein noodles in bottom of 2-quart serving dish. Top with seafood mixture. Garnish with toasted almonds. Serve hot.   4 TO 5 SERVINGS

   Tips: *One kind of seafood or two different kinds can be used. We particularly like a combination of tuna and crab for this dish.
   **Cream of asparagus or other condensed cream soups can be used for the cream of chicken soup.

Broiled Salmon Steaks with Zippy Italian Sauce, above

Golden Fried Fish Menu

Golden Fried Fish
Quick Potato Browns, page 105
Saucy Italian Beans, page 97
Fruit Salads on Lettuce
Beverage
Peach Glory Coffee Cake, page 119
MENU PREPARATION TIME: 45 MIN.

SUGGESTED ALTERNATES

Potato: A potato dish that needs no gravy, such as Double Tasty Potato Fry, page 105, or a mashed potato casserole, page 106.

Vegetable: A green or other colorful vegetable, such as Caesar's Asparagus, page 94 or Spinach Elegant, page 102.

Dessert: Something sweet and chewy — like Apple Cinnamon upside down cake, page 120, or Pumpkin Pie Cake, page 120.

Purchasing fish already filleted or cut into steaks makes preparation easy. A few herb additions to the breading in this recipe add an interesting twist.

Approximately 15 min.
GOLDEN FRIED FISH

2 lbs. fish fillets or steaks*
1 cup cracker meal, toasted bread crumbs or cornmeal
2 teaspoons parsley flakes
¼ teaspoon ground thyme, if desired
¼ cup milk or 1 egg beaten with 2 tablespoons water
Salt
Pepper

Wash and dry fish. In shallow pan or plastic bag combine cracker meal, parsley flakes and thyme. Mix well. Dip fish in milk, then coat in cracker meal mixture. In a large fry pan, fry fish in hot oil or shortening until crisp and golden on underside, about 2 to 3 minutes. Turn carefully and quickly brown other side, cooking until fish flakes easily with a fork. Drain on paper toweling. Transfer to a heated platter. Season with salt and pepper. Garnish with lemon wedges and serve with tartar sauce.

4 SERVINGS

Elegance in a jiffy — a great recipe for entertaining or special occasions. Patty shells or toast points make nice serving bases. Tasty for luncheon or dinner.

Approximately 15 min.
LOBSTER NEWBERG

4 tablespoons butter or margarine
1½ tablespoons flour
2 cups cooked lobster meat, cut into chunks*
¼ cup sherry or white wine
½ teaspoon salt
Dash paprika
2 egg yolks, slightly beaten
1½ cups light cream**

In top of double boiler or over very low heat, melt butter. Stir in flour. Add lobster, sherry, salt and paprika. In small mixing bowl, combine beaten egg yolks and cream. Add to lobster mixture and blend well. Cook over very low heat, stirring frequently, until thickened. Serve at once over toast points.   4 SERVINGS

Tips:*Cooked crabmeat or shrimp can be used for the lobster.
**If desired, 1⅓ cups milk plus 2 tablespoons butter or margarine can be used for the light cream.

Approximately 20 min.
GARLIC BROILED SHRIMP

2 lbs. fresh shrimp*
½ cup butter or margarine, melted
½ teaspoon garlic powder
1 tablespoon parsley flakes
½ teaspoon salt

Preheat broiler. Shell and devein raw shrimp. Arrange in greased baking pan. In small saucepan, melt butter. Add garlic powder, parsley flakes and salt. Brush half of garlic butter over shrimp. Broil 4 inches from heat for 6 to 8 minutes. Turn, brush with remaining garlic butter; broil 6 to 8 minutes.

4 SERVINGS

Tips: *Frozen prepared shrimp can be used for the fresh. Broiling time will be slightly less. Shrimp can be threaded on skewers and placed 8 to 10 inches from heat on outdoor grill. Brush with garlic butter while grilling.

Eggs and Cheese

This Mexican dish is easy on the budget as well as your time. A marinated salad and refried beans (or your choice of vegetable) make it a good supper menu.

Approximately 20 min.

CHILIS RELLENOS

    6 (two 4-oz. cans) whole green chilis
    2 oz. Monterey Jack or American cheese
    1 egg
    3 tablespoons flour
    2 tablespoons butter or margarine

Sauce:

    1 cup (8-oz. can) tomatoes or stewed tomatoes
    1 tablespoon flour
    1 teaspoon instant minced onion or 2 tablespoons chopped onion

Gently rinse chilis and remove any remaining seeds from center. HANDLE CHILIS GENTLY TO AVOID TEARING. Place on paper towel to dry. Cut cheese into strips about ½-inch thick and 3-inches long. Stuff centers of chilis with strips of cheese. In small mixing bowl, beat egg until frothy. Add flour; continue beating until mixture is thick. Heat butter in large fry pan on low heat. Dip stuffed chilis into egg mixture to coat. Immediately place in fry pan. Fry on both sides until coating is set and cheese has melted, about 5 minutes. Prepare Sauce while chilis are cooking. Serve chilis hot with Sauce.

Sauce: In small saucepan, combine all ingredients. Cook on medium heat until mixture thickens and comes to a boil. Reduce heat; keep warm until chilis are ready.

3 SERVINGS

Tip: For spicier Sauce, add ½ teaspoon chili powder before cooking.

This very attractive omelet gets its height from beating the egg whites separately. Canadian bacon and a sweet roll would make it a lovely brunch menu.

Approximately 30 min.

PUFFY OMELET WITH CHEESE SAUCE

    6 eggs, separated
    ⅓ cup light cream or milk
    ¼ teaspoon salt
    Dash pepper
    2 tablespoons butter or margarine

Cheese Sauce:

    1 package (1½ oz.) white sauce mix
    1 cup milk
    ½ cup cubed American cheese
    ¼ teaspoon dry mustard
    Dash pepper

Preheat oven to 375°. In large mixer bowl, beat egg whites until soft peaks form. In small mixing bowl, beat egg yolks with milk, salt and pepper. Fold yolk mixture into beaten whites. In large fry pan, melt butter. Add omelet mixture. Cook over very low heat 5 to 10 minutes until bottom is set. (Wrap plastic handle with aluminum foil.) Bake at 375° for 8 to 10 minutes, until top is light golden brown. Fold and turn out on hot platter. Spoon Cheese Sauce over omelet.

Cheese Sauce: In small saucepan, combine sauce mix and milk. Add cheese cubes, mustard and pepper. Cook over low heat, stirring constantly, until thickened and cheese is melted.

3 TO 4 SERVINGS

Tip: Cheese sauce mix, prepared according to package directions can be used for Cheese Sauce recipe.

This delicately flavored cheese pie is a French favorite. Serve it with a large salad and crunchy rolls for a great luncheon or supper meal.

Approximately 45 min.

QUICHE LORRAINE

- 1 can (8 oz.) Pillsbury Refrigerated Quick Crescent Dinner Rolls
- 1 egg, beaten
- 1 cup evaporated milk
- ½ teaspoon salt
- ½ teaspoon Worcestershire sauce
- 1 cup shredded Swiss cheese
- 1 cup (3½-oz. can) French-fried onions, if desired
- 9 slices crisp bacon, crumbled

Preheat oven to 325°. Separate dough into 8 triangles. Place dough in ungreased 9-inch pie pan (or 9-inch quiche pan), pressing pieces together to form a crust. In medium mixing bowl, combine egg, milk, salt and Worcestershire sauce. Stir in cheese. Sprinkle half of onions over unbaked crust. Pour egg mixture into crust. Sprinkle with bacon and remaining onions. Bake at 325° for 25 to 30 minutes until set (40 to 45 minutes for quiche pan). Allow to cool 5 minutes before serving. 9-INCH PIE

Tip: If desired, 1 cup diced ham can be used for the bacon.

Approximately 25 min.

WELSH RAREBIT

- 2 tablespoons butter or margarine
- 2 cups (1 lb.) cubed American cheese
- 1 cup beer
- 2 eggs, slightly beaten
- 1 teaspoon dry mustard
- 1 teaspoon Worcestershire sauce
- 4 drops Tabasco sauce, if desired
- 4 slices toast

In medium saucepan over low heat, melt butter. Add cheese and beer. Cook over very low heat until cheese melts. In small mixing bowl, combine beaten egg, dry mustard, Worcestershire sauce and Tabasco sauce. Add slowly to melted cheese, beating with a wire whisk or rotary beater. Continue cooking, stirring occasionally, about 10 minutes, until thickened. Serve over toast points.

4 SERVINGS

Canned soup adds a quick twist to scrambled eggs. Easy and inexpensive for breakfast, lunch, or supper. For a complete meal serve with broccoli, toast or rolls, and a fruity salad.

Approximately 20 min.

MUSHROOM-SCRAMBLED EGGS

- ¼ cup butter or margarine
- 10 to 12 eggs, beaten
- ¼ cup chopped green pepper, green onion or chives
- 1¼ cups (10½-oz. can) condensed cream of mushroom soup
- ½ teaspoon salt

In large fry pan or electric fry pan, melt butter over low heat. In large mixing bowl, combine remaining ingredients; mix well. Add to hot fry pan. Cook slowly, stirring occasionally from outside edge toward center (allow uncooked egg in center to flow to outside), until eggs are thickened and cooked. Serve hot. 8 TO 10 SERVINGS

Tip: For Cheesy Eggs, omit soup; add 1 cup (4 oz.) shredded or cubed Cheddar, American or pasteurized process cheese to eggs before scrambling.

Try a new flavor in your pancakes. Sausage and fruit make a whole meal out of them.

Approximately 20 min.

TIME-OUT TREATS

- 2 cups Pillsbury Hungry Jack Buttermilk or Extra Lights Pancake Mix
- 1 cup mashed ripe banana

Prepare pancake batter as directed on package, adding mashed banana with dry mix. Cook as directed. Serve warm with Brown Sugar Topping.

Brown Sugar Topping: Cream ½ cup butter until light and fluffy. Gradually add ½ cup brown sugar and beat until well blended. Stir in 1 teaspoon grated orange rind.

18 TO 20 4-INCH PANCAKES

Eggs Benedict, below

The hollandaise sauce mix makes this colorful and tasty dish very easy. It's a meal-in-one dish!

Approximately 20 min.

EGGS BENEDICT

- 4 eggs
- 1 package (1¼ oz.) hollandaise sauce mix
- ¾ cup milk
- 2 English muffins, split and toasted
- 2 tablespoons butter or margarine
- 4 slices cooked ham or Canadian bacon

*Fill large fry pan with at least 1½ inches of water. Add ¼ teaspoon salt. Bring just to a boil. Break eggs, one at a time, into a saucer and slip into simmering water. Cover. Reduce heat and cook 3 to 5 minutes, to desired doneness. In small saucepan, combine sauce mix and milk. Cook as directed on sauce mix package. Butter English muffins and arrange on serving plate. Place a slice of ham on each muffin; top with poached eggs. Cover with hollandaise sauce. Serve immediately.

4 SERVINGS

Tip: *Eggs can be poached in an egg poacher, if desired.

Approximately 25 min.

PANCAKES DIVAN

- 2 cups Pillsbury Hungry Jack Buttermilk or Extra Lights Pancake Mix
- 2 eggs
- 1 cup water
- ¼ cup oil or melted shortening
- 1½ cups (10-oz. pkg.) frozen asparagus spears

Mushroom Cheese Sauce:
- 1¼ cups (10½-oz. can) condensed cream of mushroom soup
- ⅓ cup milk
- 1½ cups (6 oz.) shredded cheese

In medium mixing bowl, combine eggs, water and oil. Add pancake mix; stir until large lumps disappear. Cook pancakes as directed on package. Meanwhile, cook asparagus according to package directions. Arrange asparagus spears on top of pancakes. Top with Mushroom Cheese Sauce.

Mushroom Cheese Sauce: Combine cream of mushroom soup with milk. Stir in shredded cheese. Heat, stirring occasionally, over low heat until cheese is melted.

4 TO 6 SERVINGS

You can keep the ingredients for this supper dish on your shelves for anytime use. Make it extra hearty by adding meat. Serve with a crisp salad like coleslaw for a tasty lunch or supper.

Pictured on page 10
Approximately 30 min.

TOMATO MACARONI AND CHEESE

1¼ cups (10-oz. can) condensed tomato soup

1 cup water

¼ cup butter or margarine

1 teaspoon parsley flakes or chopped parsley, if desired

1 package (7¼ oz.) macaroni and cheese sauce mix

Combine all ingredients, plus sauce mix from package *and* macaroni. Bring to simmer. Simmer, stirring frequently, for 15 to 20 minutes until macaroni is tender and most of liquid has been absorbed. Serve hot. 4 TO 5 SERVINGS

Tip: For extra hearty dish, add 2 cups cubed ham, 8 strips cooked crumbled bacon, or 2 cups (12-oz. can) luncheon meat, cut into strips, to macaroni mixture after macaroni is tender. Heat until heated through.

This yummy omelet made in a fry pan makes an appetizing breakfast, lunch or supper. Toast and fruit round out the flavors nicely.

Approximately 20 min.

BACON-CHEESE OMELET

4 slices bacon

4 eggs

¼ cup milk

Dash pepper

1 cup (4 oz.) shredded Cheddar or American cheese

Fry bacon in fry pan until crisp. Drain; reserve 3 tablespoons drippings. Crumble bacon. Wipe fry pan so no particles remain; return drippings to it. Place over low to medium heat. Beat eggs, milk and pepper until blended; pour into hot fry pan. Lift edges of omelet as it cooks, allowing uncooked egg to flow to bottom of fry pan. Do not stir. When eggs are set, top with bacon and cheese. Cover fry pan until cheese melts. Fold omelet; turn out on hot platter and serve immediately. 4 SERVINGS

BREAKFAST IDEAS

• Serve fried or poached eggs on slices of ham or Canadian-style bacon and top with a mustard sauce.

• Scramble eggs with crisp-crumbled bacon, flavored croutons, cubed or grated cheese, crushed herbs or chopped onion or green pepper and chopped ham or luncheon meat.

• Fold a puffy omelet and fill with chopped ham or green pepper; top with tomato or cheese sauce.

• Bake eggs in mashed potato cups; tomato shells, green pepper halves or rings.

• Poach eggs in cheese sauce, creole sauce or slightly diluted canned soup such as celery, potato or asparagus.

• Heat preserves or jam and serve over waffles or pancakes.

Great for a brunch or lunch, this take-off on crepes has a company-good flavor. Serve with fruit or a green vegetable.

Approximately 25 min.

MUSHROOM CHEESE BRUNCHCAKES

1 cup Pillsbury Hungry Jack Buttermilk Pancake Mix

½ cup (2 oz.) shredded sharp Cheddar cheese

Mushroom-Cheese Topper:

1 can (4 oz. can) drained and chopped mushroom stems and pieces

¼ cup butter or margarine

1 package (8 oz.) cream cheese

⅔ cup milk

Preheat broiler. Prepare and bake pancakes as directed on package. Fold each pancake in half and fill with 1 tablespoon Mushroom-Cheese Topper. Arrange in 9-inch square pan. Pour remaining topping over pancakes. Top with shredded cheese. Broil 3 to 4 minutes until bubbly.

Mushroom-Cheese Topper: In small fry pan, sauté chopped mushrooms in butter for 5 minutes. Add cream cheese and stir over low heat until melted. Stir in milk. Heat thoroughly.
3 TO 4 SERVINGS

Swiss Cheese Fondue
French Bread
Caesar Salad, page 87
Beverage
Cherry Crisp, page 121
MENU PREPARATION TIME: 1 HR.

Buttermilk Waffles
Fruit Butters
Brown and Serve Sausages
Fruit Salad Arrangement, page 91
Milk
MENU PREPARATION TIME: 30 MIN.

SUGGESTED ALTERNATES

Salad: Any crisp and colorful combination of greens and vegetables, page 89.

Dessert: Something fruity and sweet — maybe Strawberries Deluxe, page 116, Sherry Broiled Grapefruit, page 114, or Double Delight Fruit Cup, page 119.

TIME HELPS: Put the Cherry Crisp in the oven to bake, then marinate the garlic in oil for the salad. Meanwhile cut the bread into cubes and start the fondue. The beverage and salad greens can be prepared last, waiting just before serving to toss the salad with the dressing.

The Cherry Crisp can cool slightly while you eat the fondue — a flavorful Swiss-inspired meal with fun for all.

Approximately 20 min.
SWISS CHEESE FONDUE
¾ cup dry white wine* (sauterne)
⅛ teaspoon garlic powder
4 cups (1 lb.) shredded natural Swiss cheese
2 tablespoons flour
⅛ teaspoon ground nutmeg
¼ teaspoon salt
Dash pepper
1 loaf crusty French bread

In large bowl or plastic bag, sprinkle flour, nutmeg, salt and pepper over shredded cheese. Toss to coat cheese thoroughly. Heat wine and garlic powder in chafing dish over direct flame until wine begins to bubble. Add about ¼ cup cheese mixture; stir vigorously. Continue adding cheese in small amounts and stirring until all the cheese is melted and mixture is thoroughly blended. Serve immediately with bite-size pieces of bread dipped into the fondue.

SUGGESTED ALTERNATES

Sausages: Try bacon, Canadian bacon, fried scrapple or ham slices.

Fruit: Any kind of fruit, fruit combination or fruit juice.

Beverage: Chocolate milk, eggnog, tea or coffee.

TIME HELPS: Prepare fruit and butters and place in refrigerator until ready. Next, mix waffle batter and begin cooking. While waffles are cooking, prepare sausages.

A quick supper, lunch or brunch idea that's easy to fix and very inexpensive to serve. Different whipped butters and toppings let you serve it with a flair.

Approximately 15 min.
BUTTERMILK WAFFLES
1¾ cups Pillsbury All Purpose Flour
2 teaspoons baking powder
½ teaspoon soda
½ teaspoon salt
2 cups buttermilk or sour milk*
3 eggs
½ cup oil or melted shortening

In large mixing bowl, combine flour, baking powder, soda and salt. In small mixing bowl, combine buttermilk, eggs and oil. Beat with a rotary beater until smooth. Add liquid ingredients to flour mixture and beat just until smooth. Bake in preheated waffle iron at medium heat until steaming stops and waffle is golden brown. Serve immediately.

4 SERVINGS

Tip: Sour milk can be made by adding 2 tablespoons vinegar or lemon juice to 2 cups milk. Stir; allow to stand 10 minutes until soured.

Buttermilk Waffle Menu

Egg Foo Yong
Quick Fried Rice, page 107
Sweet Sour Vegetables, page 104
Crunchy Cabbage Salad, page 88
Tea
Quick Coconut Delights, page 117
MENU PREPARATION TIME: 1 HR.

SUGGESTED ALTERNATES

Vegetables: A colorful vegetable, such as Caesar's Asparagus, page 94, Sherried Carrots, page 99, or Cheesy Crumb Tomatoes, page 102.

Salad: Fruit Slaw, page 91, Carrot Orange Toss, page 90, or a quick molded gelatin salad would be good.

Dessert: Something with a coconut or almond flavor — maybe Almond Bear Claws, page 118, or Toasted Coconut Sundae Squares, page 114.

TIME HELPS: Bake the cookies first so they can be cooling until time for dessert. In between various batches of cookies, prepare the salad, waiting until the last minute to add crunchy ingredients. (If you don't have leftover cooked rice to use in the fried rice, prepare the specified amount of quick-cooking rice.)

Next, fry the bacon for the fried rice and make the sauce for the vegetables. Set the sauce aside until later, while you prepare the fried rice and then the Egg Foo Yong. About 5 minutes before serving, sauté the vegetables and add the sauce.

Add the remaining ingredients to the salad and serve this Far Eastern-inspired meal with chopsticks or forks and tea.

Great for a dinner or supper with an Oriental flair — a good budget-stretcher, too. Try it for a casual entertaining idea or a family meal.

Approximately 20 min.
EGG FOO YONG
  6 eggs
  1½ cups (16-oz. can) drained bean sprouts
  ¼ cup instant minced onion or 1 cup chopped onion
  2 tablespoons chopped green pepper
  ½ teaspoon salt
  Dash pepper

In large mixing bowl, beat eggs well. Add remaining ingredients and mix well. In large fry pan, heat about 2 tablespoons oil. Drop egg mixture by tablespoonfuls; fry until golden. Turn and brown other side. Drain on paper towel, if desired. Add oil to fry pan if necessary and continue to cook the remaining egg mixture. Serve hot with soy sauce, if desired.
                              4 TO 6 SERVINGS

  Tip: Sliced water chestnuts, diced cooked pork or shrimp can be added for variety.

Egg Foo Yong Menu

Soups and Sandwiches

Approximately 15 min.

BROILER TUNA BUNS

¾ cup (6½-oz. can) drained tuna

1 cup (4 oz.) shredded sharp Cheddar cheese

2 tablespoons chopped onion

2 tablespoons chopped pickle relish

½ cup mayonnaise or salad dressing

Dash salt and pepper

In small mixing bowl, combine all ingredients, mix well. Spread on 6 to 8 hamburger bun halves. Sprinkle with parsley flakes, if desired. Place on broiler pan, 6 inches from heat. Broil 3 to 5 minutes until hot and bubbly. Serve hot.   4 SERVINGS

A great family sandwich. The flavors have an overall effect much like French toast and sausage.

Approximately 15 min.

FRENCH TOASTED SANDWICH

4 eggs

½ cup milk

Dash salt and pepper

8 slices white bread

1 can (12 oz.) luncheon meat, cut into 8 slices

2 tablespoons oil or shortening

In shallow dish beat eggs and milk together. Season with salt and pepper. Lay two slices luncheon meat on each of 4 pieces of bread. Cover with remainder of bread slices. Dip each side of sandwich into egg mixture and coat well. In large fry pan, brown sandwiches on both sides. Serve with maple syrup.

    4 SERVINGS

Tip: Ham or salami can be used for the luncheon meat, if desired.

Approximately 25 min.

MANHATTAN CLAM CHOWDER

1¼ cups (10¼-oz. can) frozen cream of potato soup or condensed cream of potato soup

1 cup (8-oz. can) undrained clams

1 cup (8-oz. can) stewed tomatoes

¼ cup chopped celery

1 teaspoon instant minced onion

In saucepan, combine potato soup, clams, stewed tomatoes, diced celery and minced onion. Cover. Simmer 15 to 20 minutes until heated, stirring occasionally. If desired, garnish with parsley flakes.   4 TO 6 SERVINGS

Tip: For New England Clam Chowder, omit stewed tomatoes. Add ½ cup water and 1 teaspoon parsley flakes.

A barbecue treat that's full of hidden flavor extras.

Approximately 20 min.

FILLED TREASUREBURGERS

2 lbs. ground beef

2 teaspoons salt

¼ teaspoon pepper

2 packages (⅝-oz. each) Pillsbury Brown Gravy Mix

½ cup (2 oz.) shredded Cheddar cheese

14-inch loaf French or Italian Bread

1 tomato, sliced

Preheat broiler. Combine beef, salt, pepper and 1 package of gravy mix; blend well. Shape meat mixture into four 9x4-inch rectangles. Sprinkle cheese and remaining package of gravy mix over two rectangles. Place tomato slice on top of each. Top each with a remaining rectangle of meat and press edges together. Broil or grill on both sides until of desired doneness. Cut the loaf of bread in half, then split each half lengthwise. Serve one treasureburger on each half; cut into serving portions.   4 TO 6 SERVINGS

Homemade potato soup that's streamlined by using mashed potato flakes. Serve it piping hot or chilled.

Approximately 20 min.
POTATO POTAGE
2 tablespoons instant minced onion or ½ cup chopped onion

¼ cup butter or margarine

3 chicken bouillon cubes

2 cups boiling water

1 cup Pillsbury Hungry Jack Mashed Potato Flakes

¼ to ½ teaspoon salt

¼ teaspoon garlic salt

1 cup heavy cream

2 drops hot pepper sauce

Sauté onions in butter until golden brown in saucepan. Dissolve bouillon cubes in boiling water. Add to onions. Cover and cook 15 minutes. Press through a sieve. Add potato flakes, salt, and garlic salt to liquid, stirring lightly with a fork. Add cream and hot pepper sauce; heat thoroughly but do not boil. Garnish with croutons or chives.   3½ CUPS SOUP

Tip: If desired, serve chilled. Spoon off butter. Garnish with chives.

Prepared soups are made extra hearty in this combination. Great for cool weather.

Approximately 10 min.
CREAMY VEGETABLE SOUP
1¼ cups (10¼-oz. can) condensed potato soup

1¼ cups (10-oz. can) beef bouillon*

1¼ cups water

1½ cups (10-oz. pkg.) frozen mixed vegetables

In medium saucepan, combine all ingredients; mix well. Heat over medium heat until heated through. Serve hot with croutons or crackers.

4 TO 6 SERVINGS

Tips: *If desired, 1¼ cups water and 2 beef bouillon cubes or 2 teaspoons instant bouillon can be used for the canned bouillon.

Chicken bouillon can be used for the beef.

Approximately 15 min.
SEAFOOD BISQUE
2 tablespoons instant minced onion

¾ cup (6½-oz. can) tuna, drained*

1¼ cups (10½-oz. can) condensed cream of celery soup

1¼ cups (10½-oz. can) condensed vegetarian vegetable soup

1 teaspoon parsley flakes

In saucepan, combine all ingredients. Stir to blend. Cover. Simmer for 10 to 15 minutes to heat well.   4 TO 6 SERVINGS

Tips: *If desired, 1 cup flaked salmon, crabmeat or clams can be used for the tuna.

Approximately 1 hr.
SPEEDY HOMEMADE CHICKEN SOUP
2½ to 3 lbs. stewing chicken, cut-up

1 cup (1 lg.) carrot slices

1 cup (2 stalks) sliced celery

2 tablespoons instant minced onion or ½ cup chopped onion

6 cups water

2 teaspoons salt

⅛ teaspoon pepper

1 teaspoon parsley flakes

1 to 2 cups egg noodles or 1 cup quick-cooking rice

In pressure cooker, combine chicken, carrot, celery, onion, water, salt, pepper and parsley flakes. Close cover securely. Place pressure regulator in vent pipe and cook until 15 pounds pressure is reached or pressure regulator is rocking slowly. Reduce heat and cook at 15 pounds of pressure for 15 minutes. Remove from heat. Let pressure cooker stand, allowing pressure to drop by itself. Remove chicken. Add noodles or rice; cover and simmer 15 minutes until done. While noodles are cooking, remove meat from bones, cut into bite-size pieces and return to soup.

6 SERVINGS

Tip: To make without pressure cooker, use 5 cups (four 10¼-oz. cans) chicken broth and 2 cups (two 7-oz. cans) boned chicken. Omit water. Combine all ingredients; simmer, covered, over medium heat for 15 minutes until vegetables and noodles are tender.

French Onion Soup and Reuben Sandwich, opposite page

Approximately 30 min.
FRENCH ONION SOUP

    3 large onions, sliced

    4 tablespoons butter or margarine

    4 cups water

    6 beef bouillon cubes

    1 teaspoon Worcestershire sauce

    ½ teaspoon paprika

    Dash pepper

    Slices of toasted crusty French bread,
    if desired

    Grated Parmesan cheese, if desired

In large deep fry pan, cook onions in butter until golden. Add water, bouillon cubes, Worcestershire sauce, paprika and pepper. Simmer 15 to 20 minutes. To serve, top with a slice of toasted French bread and sprinkle with grated Parmesan cheese.

                    4 TO 6 SERVINGS

Approximately 10 min.
REUBEN SANDWICH

    2 cups (12-oz. can) shredded corned beef

    ¼ cup chopped green pepper

    2 tablespoons catsup

    1 teaspoon cream-style horseradish,
    if desired

    ¾ cup (8-oz. can) well-drained sauerkraut

    ½ teaspoon caraway seeds

    1 cup (4 oz.) shredded Swiss cheese

    4 rolls, split

Combine corned beef, green pepper, catsup, horseradish and mix thoroughly. Spoon onto one side of rolls. Top with sauerkraut; sprinkle with caraway seeds. Top with cheese. Place top half of roll on sandwich. 4 SANDWICHES

Approximately 15 min.
POTAGE ST. GERMAIN

    2 cups water

    1¼ cups (10-oz. can) condensed pea soup
    or frozen pea soup

    ½ cup (1 med.) grated carrot

    2 chicken bouillon cubes or 2 teaspoons
    instant bouillon

    ½ teaspoon sugar

    ¼ teaspoon mint leaves, if desired

In medium saucepan, combine all ingredients. Bring to a boil. Reduce heat; simmer 5 to 10 minutes until carrots are tender. Garnish with croutons to serve.   4 SERVINGS

Approximately 20 min.
HAM AND CHEESEWICHES

    1 can (8 oz.) Pillsbury Refrigerated
    Quick Crescent Dinner Rolls

    8 slices ready-to-eat ham

    4 slices pasteurized process cheese,
    cut in half

    Catsup or prepared mustard, if desired

Preheat oven to 375°. Separate dough into 4 rectangles. Place 2 slices of ham and ½ slice of cheese at one end of each. If desired, spread with catsup or mustard. Fold over. Bring edges of dough together to cover filling; fork edges to seal. Top with another ½ slice of cheese. Bake at 375° for 10 to 13 minutes. Serve hot.   4 SANDWICHES

    Tip: Corned beef slices and Swiss cheese can be substituted for ham and American cheese. If desired, spread with mustard.

Approximately 15 min.
CHILI DOGS

    8 rolls or hotdog buns

    8 (about 1 lb.) wieners

    2 cups (15¼-oz. can) chili with beans

In medium saucepan, heat weiners in chili about 10 minutes, until heated through. Split rolls lengthwise. Place a wiener and a spoonfull of chili into each roll. Serve hot.

                    8 SANDWICHES

Approximately 30 min.
BAKED CLUBHOUSE SANDWICHES

    4 slices bread, toasted

    4 large slices chicken or turkey

    4 slices ham or luncheon meat

    1¼ cups (10½-oz. can) cream of
    mushroom soup

    ¼ cup dry sherry or white wine

    Paprika

Preheat oven to 375°. Arrange toast in baking dish. Place one slice each of ham and turkey on each. In small mixing bowl, combine soup and sherry. Blend well. Pour over sandwiches. Sprinkle with paprika. Bake, uncovered, at 375° for 15 to 20 minutes until heated.

                    4 SERVINGS

    Tip: Sherry can be omitted, if desired. Use milk instead.

Meal Accompaniments

Speedy Bread Sticks, page 108, Onion Simmered Beans, page 97, French-Seasoned Vegetables, page 104, Maple Glazed Sweets, page 104 and Spicy Peach Salad, page 90.

Salads

Approximately 15 min.

BASIC SOUR CREAM COLESLAW

   1 small head cabbage, shredded or
      thinly sliced
   1½ teaspoons instant minced onion or
      2 tablespoons chopped onion
   2 tablespoons sugar
   ½ teaspoon salt
   ½ cup dairy or imitation sour cream
   1 teaspoon lemon juice

In large mixing bowl, combine all ingredients;
toss lightly. Serve immediately. 4 SERVINGS

> Tips: For a crisp chilled coleslaw,
> shredded cabbage can be chilled in ice
> water for about an hour. Drain and
> combine with remaining ingredients.
> For Coconutty Slaw, add ¼ cup sliced
> and quartered cucumber and ¼ cup
> flaked coconut to cabbage mixture; omit
> onion.
> For Fruit Slaw, add 1⅔ cups (1-lb. can)
> drained pineapple tidbits, 2 cups
> miniature marshmallows and ½ cup
> (1 stalk) chopped celery to cabbage
> mixture; omit onion. If desired, garnish
> with maraschino cherries. Serves 8.
> For Apple Slaw, add 1 large apple, cubed,
> 1 teaspoon grated orange peel,
> ⅛ teaspoon cinnamon and ⅛ teaspoon
> ground cloves to cabbage mixture; omit
> onion.

Approximately 15 min.

CRISPY ONION AND GREENS TOSS

   2 to 3 cups iceberg lettuce, torn into
      bite-size pieces
   2 to 3 cups fresh spinach, torn into
      bite-size pieces
   ½ cup French fried onion rings
   ¼ cup prepared French or other
      colorful dressing

In salad bowl, toss lettuce and spinach with
part of onion rings (reserving remainder for
garnish). Chill until ready to serve. To serve,
top with dressing and reserved onion rings.
4 TO 6 SERVINGS

Approximately 45 min.

CAESAR SALAD

   1 clove garlic, halved
   ½ cup cooking oil
   2 cups soft bread cubes
   2 heads romaine lettuce, torn into
      bite-size pieces
   ½ teaspoon salt
   Dash pepper
   1 egg
   ¼ cup lemon juice
   ¼ cup grated Parmesan cheese

Marinate garlic in oil about 30 minutes; remove
garlic. In 2 tablespoons of the oil, brown bread
cubes. If desired, rub salad bowl with clove of
garlic, discard garlic. In salad bowl, combine
lettuce, salt, pepper and remaining oil; toss
lightly. Break egg over lettuce. Add lemon juice
and toss again. Add cheese and bread cubes;
toss lightly. If desired, top with anchovy fillets.
Serve immediately.   4 TO 6 SERVINGS

A simple dressing made with vinegar and hot bacon drippings gives this salad its exceptional flavor and traditional "wilted" appearance.
Pictured on page 52

Approximately 15 min.
WILTED LETTUCE SALAD
- 5 slices bacon
- 2 hard cooked eggs, chopped
- 2 heads leaf lettuce, torn into bite-size pieces
- 2 tablespoons chopped green onion or chopped chives
- 1 tablespoon sugar
- ½ teaspoon salt
- ¼ teaspoon pepper
- ¼ cup cider vinegar
- 2 tablespoons cold water

Fry bacon until crisp. Drain on paper towels; reserve 2 tablespoons drippings. In large serving bowl, combine lettuce, onion and chopped eggs. Combine reserved 2 tablespoons bacon drippings with remaining ingredients. Heat just to boiling. Pour over lettuce; toss lightly. Garnish with crumbled bacon; serve immediately.   8 SERVINGS

Tips: For an extra zippy salad, add ¼ teaspoon dry mustard with pepper.

If desired, crumbled bleu cheese or Italian seasoning can be sprinkled over salad before serving.

A few colorful vegetables and some sugar perk up the sauerkraut to make a sweet-sour salad.

Approximately 15 min.
KRAUT SALAD
- ¾ cup (8-oz. can) drained sauerkraut
- ⅓ cup sugar
- ½ cup finely chopped green pepper
- ¼ cup (½ small) finely chopped onion or green onion
- 1 tablespoon chopped pimiento

In medium mixing bowl, combine all ingredients; mix well. Chill before serving. If desired, garnish with radish slices. 4 SERVINGS

Chinese cabbage stars in this Oriental salad. Chow mein noodles add a crunch and give an interesting combination.
Pictured on page 81

Approximately 10 min.
CRUNCHY CABBAGE SALAD
- 4 cups shredded Chinese cabbage
- ½ cup (5-oz. can) drained, sliced water chestnuts
- ½ cup (4-oz. can) drained, sliced mushrooms
- 1 tablespoon chopped onion
- ½ cup mayonnaise or salad dressing
- 1 to 2 tablespoons soy sauce
- ¾ cup chow mein noodles

In large bowl, combine cabbage, water chestnuts, mushrooms and onion. In small bowl, combine mayonnaise and soy sauce; pour over cabbage mixture. Toss lightly. Just before serving, add chow mein noodles; toss lightly. Serve immediately. If desired, garnish with toasted almonds.   6 SERVINGS

This sweet 'n sour bean salad uses ingredients you can keep on hand. Leftovers will taste just as good the next day, too.

Approximately 20 min.
BEAN O' RELISH SALAD
- 1¾ cups (1-lb. can) undrained kidney beans
- 1 medium onion, sliced
- ¼ cup sweet pickle relish
- 2 tablespoons cooking oil
- 2 tablespoons vinegar or lemon juice
- 2 tablespoons water
- 2 tablespoons sugar
- ½ teaspoon salt

In medium mixing bowl, combine all ingredients. Stir gently to combine. Chill 15 minutes or until serving time. Drain extra liquid. Serve by itself or on lettuce leaves.
          4 SERVINGS

Tip: Other kinds of beans, as well as combinations of different types of beans, can be used for the kidney beans.

VEGETABLE SALAD COMBINATIONS

Iceberg lettuce, cooked green beans, hard cooked egg slices, onion and French dressing

Romaine lettuce, grated carrot, julienne beet strips and blue cheese dressing

Spinach, romaine lettuce, hard cooked egg, crumbled bacon and Basic Vinegar and Oil Dressing, page 107

Leaf lettuce, sliced raw zucchini, cherry tomatoes, onion slices and Caesar dressing

Iceberg lettuce, cucumber pieces, croutons, green onion slices and thousand island dressing

Boston bibb lettuce, tomato wedges, cauliflowerettes and French dressing

Leaf lettuce, fresh mushroom slices, cooked cubed carrot, shoestring potatoes and garlic cheese dressing

Romaine lettuce, cooked peas, cubed Cheddar cheese and thousand island dressing

Iceberg lettuce, cauliflowerettes, black olive slices, chopped chives and Basic Vinegar and Oil Dressing, page 107

Iceberg lettuce, romaine lettuce, fresh spinach and green goddess dressing

Iceberg lettuce, artichoke hearts, chopped pimiento, green pepper strips and Italian dressing

Romaine lettuce, sliced tomatoes, avocado strips and French dressing

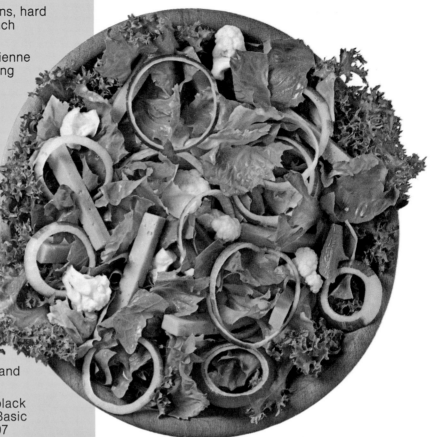

Colorful and extra easy! This is a great way to use up leftover vegetables.

Approximately 15 min.

CARROT RAISIN SALAD

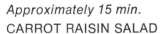

   4 medium carrots, coarsely grated

   ½ cup raisins

   ⅓ cup mayonnaise or salad dressing

   ¼ cup salted peanuts, if desired

In medium mixing bowl, combine all ingredients except peanuts; just before serving, add peanuts. If desired, garnish with additional peanuts.   4 TO 6 SERVINGS

Approximately 20 min.

SALAD MACEDOINE

   1½ cups (1-lb. can) drained mixed vegetables*

   ½ to 1 medium onion, sliced

   2 tablespoons sliced olives**

   ⅓ cup prepared French or Russian dressing

Combine all ingredients except olives. Chill in refrigerator 15 minutes or until serving time. If desired, serve on lettuce leaves. Garnish with sliced olives or onion rings. 3 TO 4 SERVINGS

   Tip: *If desired, 1½ cups (10-oz. pkg.) cooked frozen mixed vegetables can be used for the canned.

Frozen peaches and ice water, as well as individual molds, add speed to the chilling time for this gelatin salad.

Pictured on page 86
Approximately 1 hr.
SPICY PEACH SALAD
- 1 package (3 oz.) orange flavored gelatin
- ¼ teaspoon pumpkin pie spice or cinnamon
- 1 cup boiling water
- 1⅓ cups (10-oz. pkg.) frozen peach slices, unthawed
- ½ cup ice water*

In medium mixing bowl, combine dry gelatin and pumpkin pie spice. Add boiling water; stir until dissolved. Add frozen peach slices and ice water; stir until peaches are somewhat thawed and ice is melted. Pour into individual serving dishes and chill about 1 hour until firm.

4 SERVINGS

Tip: *To make ice water, fill ½ cup with ice; add water to the ½ cup measure.
Other flavors of gelatin and frozen fruit can be used for the orange gelatin and peach slices; pumpkin pie spice can be omitted. Choose your favorite combination.
Gelatin can be chilled in mold or large serving dish; however, chilling time will be longer.

Prepared salad dressing takes the work out of this salad. Western vegetables provide a new idea for marinated vegetable salads.

Approximately 20 min.
WESTERN SALAD
- 1½ cups (16-oz. can) drained garbanzo beans or chick peas
- 2 avocados, peeled and sliced
- ⅔ cup prepared Italian dressing
- Lettuce leaves
- 2 tablespoons sliced black olives
- 2 tablespoons pimiento strips

In small mixing bowl, pour dressing over beans and avocados. Chill in refrigerator for 15 minutes or until ready to serve. To serve, arrange vegetables on lettuce leaves. Garnish with olives and pimiento.   6 SERVINGS

The subtle herb flavor in these beans and dressing strikes a novel note on lettuce. A good way, too, to disguise leftover beans.

Approximately 25 min.
GREEN BEANS TARRAGON
- 2 cups (1-lb. can) drained green beans
- ¼ cup salad oil
- ¼ cup tarragon or cider vinegar
- ¼ teaspoon tarragon
- Lettuce leaves

Combine beans, oil and vinegar in bowl. Chill in refrigerator 20 minutes or until ready to serve. To serve, spoon beans and dressing over lettuce leaves on individual serving dishes. If desired, garnish with hard cooked egg slices.

4 SERVINGS

Approximately 15 min.
CREAMY FRUIT SALAD
- 4 oranges, peeled and sectioned
- 2 bananas, sliced
- 1 medium apple, chopped
- ¾ cup (8¾-oz. can) drained pineapple tidbits
- 1 cup dairy or imitation sour cream

In medium mixing bowl, combine all ingredients; toss lightly. Chill before serving. If desired, garnish with toasted almonds.

6 SERVINGS

Approximately 10 min.
CARROT ORANGE TOSS
- 2 cups (4 med.) grated carrots
- 1 cup (2 med.) orange sections*
- 3 tablespoons sugar
- ¼ cup dairy or imitation sour cream

In medium bowl, combine all ingredients; mix well. Chill until ready to serve. If desired, serve on lettuce leaves.   4 SERVINGS

Tips: *Canned or fresh orange sections can be used.
For flavor variations, grapefruit or mandarin orange sections can be used for the orange sections.

Pictured on page 43

Approximately 20 min.
QUICK FILLED PEARS

  2 cups (1 lb. 13-oz. can) drained pear
    halves
  6 tablespoons frozen or canned
    cranberry orange relish
  Lettuce leaves

Place 1 tablespoon cranberry orange relish in hollow of each pear half. On individual salad plates, arrange two filled halves on lettuce leaves. Place in refrigerator 15 minutes or until serving time.   3 SERVINGS

  Tips: Pear halves can be filled with other flavors: grated cheese, mint jelly, orange sherbet, cottage cheese, or chopped dates.
  Peach halves can be used for the pears.

Approximately 15 min.
CITRUS-AVOCADO SALAD

  1 avocado, peeled, seeded and sliced
  Lemon juice
  1 orange or 1 grapefruit, peeled and
    sectioned
  Lettuce leaves

Sprinkle avocado slices with lemon juice. On salad plates lined with lettuce leaves, alternate avocado slices and orange or grapefruit sections.   4 SERVINGS

FRUIT SALAD COMBINATIONS

Pineapple, blueberries, melon and Blender Celery Seed Dressing, page 93.

Plums, peaches, green grapes and Quick French-Russian Dressing, page 93

Banana, pineapple, dates and mayonnaise.

Raspberries, banana, coconut and Minty Fruit Dressing, page 93

Melon, pineapple, peaches and Red Raspberry Dressing, page 93

Pineapple, cherries and cottage cheese

Mandarin oranges, coconut, banana, almonds and whipped cream

Cranberries, apricots and orange sherbet

Pears, blueberries and Red Raspberry Dressing, page 93

Apples, prunes, walnuts and mayonnaise

Orange sections, banana, coconut and Honey Celery Seed Dressing, page 93

Cantaloupe, blueberries and lemon sherbet

Approximately 15 min.
FRUIT SLAW

  1 small head cabbage, shredded or
    thinly sliced
  1⅔ cups (1-lb. can) drained pineapple
    tidbits
  2 cups miniature marshmallows
  ½ cup (1 stalk) chopped celery
  1½ teaspoons instant minced onion or
    2 tablespoons chopped onion
  2 tablespoons sugar
  ½ teaspoon salt
  ½ cup dairy or imitation sour cream
  1 teaspoon lemon juice

In large bowl, combine all ingredients; toss lightly. If desired, garnish with maraschino cherries. Serve immediately. 8 SERVINGS

Combine canned potato salad with one, several, or all of the following dress-ups for fresh flavor and added interest.

Pictured on page 67

Approximately 45 min.

PANTRY POTATO SALAD

    2 cups (1-lb. can or jar) potato salad
    ¼ cup dairy or imitation sour cream
    ¼ cup cheese cubes, if desired
    ¼ cup (½ stalk) chopped celery
    2 tablespoons chopped green pepper, if desired
    2 tablespoons radish slices, if desired
    1 teaspoon prepared mustard
    ½ teaspoon celery seed, if desired

In large mixing bowl, combine all ingredients and mix well. Chill at least 30 minutes before serving. To serve, sprinkle with paprika or garnish with hard cooked egg slices or green pepper rings.   3 TO 4 SERVINGS

Tip: Other sized cans of potato salad can be used.

Potato salad is made super easy by using scalloped potato mix. Add your own favorite dress-ups for your unique touch.

Pictured on page 28

Approximately 45 min.

EASY POTATO SALAD

    1 package (5⅛ oz.) Pillsbury Scalloped Potato Mix
    ½ cup mayonnaise or salad dressing
    ¼ cup chopped onion, celery or green pepper
    Hard cooked egg
    Chopped pimiento
    1 to 2 tablespoons prepared mustard

Cook potato slices using Speedy Saucepan Method on package; drain well. Stir mayonnaise into drained potatoes. Stir in any of the following: onion, celery or green pepper; chopped hard-cooked egg; chopped pimiento or prepared mustard. If desired, thin with a few tablespoons mayonnaise or milk. Season to taste with salt and pepper. Chill 20 to 30 minutes or until ready to serve. Keep refrigerated.   4 TO 6 SERVINGS

Tip: For tarter flavor, sour cream can be used for part of the mayonnaise.

Pictured on page 32

Approximately 20 min.

WALDORF SALAD

    4 medium size apples, cubed
    ⅔ cup mayonnaise or salad dressing
    ½ cup (1 stalk) chopped celery
    ¼ cup cut-up dates
    ¼ cup chopped nuts
    2 tablespoons sugar
    1 teaspoon lemon juice

In large mixing bowl, combine all ingredients; mix well. Chill slightly before serving.
                              6 SERVINGS

Tip: For an interesting variation, add ½ cup prepared mincemeat to above recipe. Prepare as directed.

Cooling the macaroni before assembling the ingredients allows this recipe to chill in only minutes. Leftovers are just as good, too.

Pictured on page 35

Approximately 30 min.

QUICK MACARONI SALAD

    1 cup uncooked macaroni*
    ½ cup (1 stalk) chopped celery
    ¼ cup sweet pickle relish or chopped sweet pickle
    1 tablespoon chopped onion
    1 tablespoon chopped green pepper, if desired
    1 tablespoon chopped pimiento, if desired
    ¾ cup mayonnaise or salad dressing
    1 teaspoon salt

Cook macaroni in boiling, salted water until tender. Rinse in cold water until cooled; drain well. In large bowl, combine all ingredients; toss lightly. Chill 15 minutes or until ready to serve. Cook macaroni in boiling, salted water until tender. Rinse in cold water until cooled; drain well.   6 SERVINGS

Tip: *If desired, 1½ to 2 cups cooked macaroni can be used. A great way to use leftovers — and time saving, too.

This creamy dressing combines the great flavors from both French and Russian flavors. It's delicious on fresh fruit or fruit salads, lettuce salads and vegetable salads.

Approximately 5 min.

QUICK FRENCH-RUSSIAN DRESSING

⅓ cup chili sauce

¼ cup vinegar

¼ cup sugar

½ teaspoon instant minced onion or 2 teaspoons chopped onion

½ teaspoon salt

⅛ teaspoon minced garlic

½ teaspoon Worcestershire sauce

½ cup salad oil

In blender, combine all ingredients except oil. Process on medium speed until smooth. Gradually add oil through small opening in lid, continuing to process on medium speed until thoroughly combined. Store, covered, in refrigerator. Mix well before using.

1¾ CUPS DRESSING

This creamy dressing is especially easy with only 4 ingredients. It's excellent served on fresh fruit or molded gelatin salads.

Approximately 5 min.

RED RASPBERRY DRESSING

⅓ cup mayonnaise or salad dressing

⅓ cup red raspberry preserves

½ cup whipped topping or whipped cream*

¼ cup finely chopped walnuts, if desired

In small bowl, combine mayonnaise and preserves; mix well. Fold in whipped topping and walnuts. Chill before serving. Thin with a few drops of milk, if desired. Store, covered, in refrigerator. Mix well before serving.

1 CUP DRESSING

*Use ¼ cup whipping cream, whipped and sweetened to make the ½ cup whipped cream needed.

Any flavor preserves can be used for the red raspberry preserves. We especially like boysenberry and apricot.

Approximately 5 min.

BASIC VINEGAR AND OIL DRESSING

¼ to ½ cup salad oil

½ cup vinegar*

½ teaspoon salt

Dash pepper

½ teaspoon Worcestershire sauce

In blender, combine all ingredients. Process on medium speed until thoroughly combined. Store, covered, in refrigerator. Mix well before using.

1 CUP DRESSING

A sweet-sour dressing that's a great teammate for your fruit or vegetable salads. Try it heated as a glaze for some vegetables, too.

Approximately 5 min.

BLENDER CELERY SEED DRESSING

⅔ cup sugar

1 teaspoon dry mustard

1 teaspoon celery seed

1 teaspoon paprika, if desired

¼ teaspoon salt

⅓ cup vinegar

⅓ cup honey

¼ cup cold water

½ cup salad oil

In blender, combine all ingredients except oil; process on low speed until smooth. Gradually add oil through small opening in lid, continuing to process on medium speed until thick and thoroughly combined. 2 CUPS DRESSING

A honey-sour cream combination makes this dressing particularly good on fruit salads.

Approximately 5 min.

MINTY FRUIT DRESSING

1 cup dairy or imitation sour cream

2 tablespoons honey

2 tablespoons creme de menthe

¼ teaspoon salt

In small bowl, combine all ingredients; mix well. Chill before serving. Store, covered, in refrigerator. If desired, dressing can be thinned with a few drops of lemon juice before serving.

1 CUP DRESSING

Vegetables

A prepared dip gives these artichoke hearts a quick twist.

Approximately 15 min.
TANGY ARTICHOKES

1½ cups (7-oz. pkg.) frozen artichoke
    hearts
3 tablespoons prepared
    bacon-horseradish dip
1 tablespoon milk
2 tablespoons bacon-flavored bits or
    2 strips cooked crumbled bacon,
    if desired

Prepare artichokes as directed on package.
Meanwhile, mix horseradish dip and milk;
blend well. Drain water from artichokes. Add
dip mixture and bacon. Toss lightly to coat
well. Serve hot. 4 SERVINGS

*A hint of nutmeg blends the flavors of corn
and asparagus to a delight. A good way to
stretch an asparagus dish, too.*

Approximately 10 min.
ASPARAGUS CORN CUT-UP

1 cup (8-oz. can) undrained corn
1½ cups (15-oz. can) undrained
    asparagus pieces
2 tablespoons cream or milk
½ teaspoon salt
Dash ground nutmeg

In medium saucepan, heat vegetables together
in liquid from can. Drain thoroughly. Add
remaining ingredients; toss lightly to coat well.
Serve hot. 4 SERVINGS

> Tip: To use corn on the cobs, cut corn
> from cobs. Add cream, salt and nutmeg;
> simmer 5 minutes. Add drained
> asparagus; continue simmering 5 minutes
> until heated through.

*Prepared salad dressing makes an easy and
delicious addition for this asparagus dish.*

Approximately 10 min.
CAESAR'S ASPARAGUS

1½ cups (10-oz. pkg.) frozen asparagus
    pieces or spears
¼ to ⅓ cup prepared Caesar salad
    dressing
4 lemon slices

Prepare asparagus as directed on package.
Drain excess water. Add salad dressing; toss
lightly. To serve, garnish with lemon slices.
Serve hot. 4 SERVINGS

> Tip: If desired, 1½ cups (1-lb. can)
> drained asparagus pieces can be used
> for the frozen. Heat asparagus in canned
> liquid; prepare as directed.

A quick perk-up for canned pork and beans.

Approximately 40 min.
ZIPPY PORK & BEANS

½ cup (4-oz. can) deviled ham*
2 cups (1-lb. can) pork and beans
    in tomato sauce
¼ cup firmly packed brown sugar
2 teaspoons instant minced onion
    or 2 tablespoons chopped onion
1 teaspoon leaf oregano
¼ teaspoon garlic salt
¼ cup catsup

In small saucepan, combine all ingredients.
Cook, stirring occasionally, over medium heat
for 25 to 30 minutes until bubbly and heated
through. 4 SERVINGS

> Tip: *If desired, ½ cup leftover cubed
> ham can be used for the deviled ham.

The great flavor combination and fry pan method in this casserole is bound to please your family, as well as save you time.

Approximately 30 min.
LIMA-CHEESE CASSEROLE

- 3 cups (two 10-oz. pkgs.) frozen lima beans
- 4 slices bacon or ½ cup bacon flavored bits
- 2 tablespoons instant minced onion or ½ cup (1 small) chopped onion
- 1¼ cups (10 ¾-oz. can) condensed Cheddar cheese soup
- ½ cup dairy or imitation sour cream
- ¼ cup dry bread crumbs
- 1 tablespoon butter or margarine, melted

Cook beans as directed on package; drain well. In same saucepan, fry bacon until crisp; drain on paper towel; reserve drippings. In reserved bacon drippings, sauté onion until tender. Stir in cheese soup and sour cream. Add beans and crumbled bacon; mix well. Continue cooking until heated through. Brown bread crumbs in butter. To serve, top beans with toasted crumbs.   6 SERVINGS

Tip: If desired, 1⅔ cups (16-oz. can) drained lima beans can be used for the frozen beans.

Great flavored beans are ready in less than the usual time with these "on-hand" ingredients. A favorite you can pull from your pantry any time.
Pictured on page 28
Approximately 40 min.
SKILLET BAKED BEANS

- 3½ cups (two 1-lb. cans) baked beans in tomato sauce
- 6 slices bacon, cut-up
- ¼ cup catsup
- 2 tablespoons molasses
- 1 teaspoon instant minced onion
- 1 teaspoon prepared mustard

In large fry pan, fry bacon until crisp. Drain well, reserving 2 tablespoons of the bacon drippings. Add remaining ingredients; mix well. Simmer, uncovered, 20 to 30 minutes, until sauce has thickened.   4 TO 6 SERVINGS

Preseasoned bread stuffing cubes contribute their savory spices to this interesting dish.

Approximately 15 min.
SAVORY GREEN BEANS

- 2 cups (1-lb. can) undrained cut green beans
- 1 tablespoon butter or margarine
- 1 teaspoon vinegar
- 2 to 3 tablespoons grated Parmesan cheese
- 1 cup herb seasoned bread stuffing

In small saucepan, heat beans in canned liquid; drain well. Add butter. Place in serving dish and sprinkle with vinegar. Add Parmesan cheese and bread stuffing; toss lightly. Serve immediately.   4 SERVINGS

Tip: A 10-oz. package frozen cut green beans can be used for canned beans. Cook beans as directed on package; prepare as directed above.

Dill and sour cream make a tasty combination for these green beans. A fancy way to serve them in only minutes.

Approximately 10 min.
DILLY GREEN BEANS

- 1½ cups (10-oz. pkg.) frozen green beans
- ⅓ cup dairy sour cream
- 1 teaspoon instant minced onion, if desired
- 1 teaspoon dill weed or ½ teaspoon dill seed
- ½ teaspoon salt
- Dash pepper

Prepare beans as directed on package. Drain. Add remaining ingredients. Toss lightly to blend well. Serve hot.   4 SERVINGS

Tips: If desired, 1⅔ cups (1-lb. can) green beans can be used for the frozen beans. Heat in canned liquid. Drain; proceed as directed.

Fresh green beans can also be used in this recipe. Cook beans in small amount of salted water for 15 to 20 minutes until tender. Drain; proceed as directed.

Green Bean Casserole, opposite page

An easy, special fix-up for beans that uses ingredients you can keep on hand for unexpected guests.

Approximately 45 min.
GREEN BEAN CASSEROLE

- 1¾ cups (9-oz. pkg.) frozen French-style green beans
- ⅔ to 1¼ cups (half to entire 10½-oz. can) condensed cream of mushroom soup
- ½ cup French fried onions

Preheat oven to 350°. Cook beans as directed on package; drain well. In 1-quart casserole, combine beans with mushroom soup. Bake at 350° for 20 to 25 minutes until bubbly. Top with French fried onions during last 5 minutes of baking or use as a garnish. 4 SERVINGS

> Tips: If desired, 1¾ cups (1-lb. can) drained French-style green beans can be used for the frozen beans.
>
> As a variation, add ½ cup (5-oz. can) drained and sliced water chestnuts and ¼ teaspoon soy sauce to casserole. Top with chow mein noodles before or after baking as directed.
>
> If desired, top with shoestring potatoes, potato chips or crumbled cheese crackers.

Pictured on page 72
Approximately 15 min.
SAUCY ITALIAN BEANS

- 1½ cups (9-oz. pkg.) frozen Italian beans
- ½ to 1 cup (half to entire 8-oz. can) tomato sauce
- 1 teaspoon instant minced onion or 1 tablespoon chopped onion
- ⅛ teaspoon Italian seasoning, leaf oregano or thyme
- ¼ cup (2 oz.) shredded Mozzarella cheese

Cook beans as directed on package; drain well. Add remaining ingredients except cheese. Heat through, stirring occasionally. Place in serving dish and top with cheese; cover and let stand a few minutes until cheese is melted. Serve immediately. 4 SERVINGS

> Tip: If desired, 2 tablespoons grated Parmesan cheese can be used for the Mozzarella cheese.

Quick soup mix adds a tasty, creative touch to an every day vegetable. Ready any time with "on-hand" ingredients.

Pictured on page 86
Approximately 5 min.
ONION SIMMERED BEANS

- 2 cups (1-lb. can) undrained whole green beans
- 1 to 2 tablespoons dry onion soup mix

Place undrained beans in small saucepan; add onion soup mix. Heat through; drain liquid. Serve hot. 4 SERVINGS

Approximately 15 min.
BACON FRIED BEANS

- 3 slices bacon
- 1½ cups (1-lb. can) drained whole or cut green beans*
- ½ teaspoon salt
- ⅛ teaspoon pepper

In medium saucepan, fry bacon until crisp. Drain on paper towel, reserving bacon drippings. To reserved drippings, add remaining ingredients. Cook over medium heat about 5 minutes, stirring occasionally, until heated through. Sprinkle with crumbled bacon. Serve immediately. 4 TO 5 SERVINGS

> Tip: *To use frozen beans for the canned, prepare as directed, cooking beans for 8 to 10 minutes to allow for thawing.

Approximately 10 min.
CONFETTI BEANS

- 1½ cups (9-oz. pkg.) frozen wax beans
- ½ to 1 package (3 oz.) low calorie or regular cream cheese, cubed
- ¼ cup chopped green pepper
- 2 tablespoons chopped pimiento

Cook beans as directed on package; drain well. Add remaining ingredients; mix well. Serve immediately. 4 SERVINGS

> Tips: A combination of wax beans and green beans can be used.
>
> A 1 lb. can wax beans, drained, can be used for the frozen beans. Prepare as directed.

Cauliflower cooked in bouillon gives a hint of chicken flavor. Try serving it with fried chicken.

Approximately 10 min.
COUNTRY CAULIFLOWER

- ½ cup water*
- ½ teaspoon salt
- 1 chicken bouillon cube or 1 teaspoon instant bouillon
- 1½ cups (10-oz. pkg.) frozen cauliflowerettes**

In small saucepan, combine water, salt and bouillon; bring to a boil. Add frozen cauliflowerettes; bring to a boil. Reduce heat; simmer 5 to 7 minutes until tender. Drain. If desired, garnish with chopped parsley.

2 TO 3 SERVINGS

Tips: *If desired, ½ cup chicken broth can be used for the water and chicken bouillon.

**1¼ cups (¼ head) fresh cauliflower, separated into pieces, can be used for the frozen. Simmer 10 to 15 minutes until tender.

Mushrooms in a soup-based sauce lend a nice flavor to Brussels sprouts. This dish can be kept warm in the oven until serving time.

Approximately 15 min.
CREAMY SPROUTS

- 1½ cups (10-oz. pkg.) frozen Brussels sprouts
- ¾ to 1¼ cups (half to entire 10¾-oz. can) condensed cream of celery soup
- ½ cup (4-oz. can) drained mushroom stems and pieces
- ¼ cup dry bread crumbs
- 1 tablespoon butter or margarine, melted

Cook Brussels sprouts as directed on package; drain well. Add soup and mushrooms; stir gently to coat well. Continue heating 1 to 2 minutes until heated through. Meanwhile, brown bread crumbs in butter in small fry pan. To serve, top Brussels sprouts with buttered bread crumbs. 4 SERVINGS

Tip: If desired, cream of mushroom soup can be used for the cream of celery.

Approximately 20 min.
MELLOW VEGETABLE DUO

- 1 lb. fresh broccoli*
- 1 lb. (about ½ head) fresh cauliflower*
- 1 package (2¼ oz.) cheese sauce mix
- ¼ teaspoon Worcestershire sauce
- ⅛ teaspoon ground nutmeg
- 2 tablespoons buttered bread crumbs

In medium saucepan, cook broccoli and cauliflower in small amount of salted water 10 to 15 minutes until tender. Meanwhile, prepare cheese sauce mix as directed on package, adding Worcestershire sauce and nutmeg. Drain water from vegetables. Arrange in serving bowl. Top with sauce and garnish with crumbs. 6 SERVINGS

Tip: *Frozen vegetables can be used for the fresh. Two 10-oz. packages frozen equals about 1 lb. fresh.

Mellow Vegetable Duo, above

Cheese sauce mix and bacon flavored bits speed up the cooking time for this great flavored dish.

Approximately 15 min.
CHEESEY BACON BROCCOLI
    2 lbs. fresh broccoli*
    1 package (1½ oz.) cheese sauce mix
    2 tablespoons bacon-flavored bits or
      2 strips cooked and crumbled bacon

Cook broccoli in small amount of salted water. Meanwhile, prepare cheese sauce mix as directed on package, adding bacon-flavored bits after sauce has thickened. Drain broccoli; top with sauce. Serve hot.   6 SERVINGS

    Tip: *If desired, 2 packages (10-oz. each) frozen broccoli spears can be used for the fresh.

Approximately 10 min.
CARAWAY CABBAGE
    4 cups (½ med. head) coarsely shredded
      or thinly sliced cabbage
    ½ teaspoon salt
    ⅛ teaspoon pepper
    ½ teaspoon caraway
    ½ cup dairy or imitation sour cream

Wash cabbage. Place cabbage (with water that clings to the leaves), salt and pepper in saucepan. Cook, tightly covered, over medium low heat (moisture from leaves will be adequate to provide steam for cooking) 4 to 6 minutes until tender. Drain well. Add remaining ingredients to cooked cabbage. Stir to combine. If desired, top with crumbled bacon to serve. Serve immediately.   4 TO 6 SERVINGS

Vegetables that taste like they were baked with a pot roast. After you put them in the oven, they bake by themselves.

Approximately 1 hr.
OVEN BROWNED VEGETABLES
    2 large potatoes, peeled
    3 carrots, peeled
    ¾ cup (8-oz. can) drained, small whole
      onions, if desired
    3 tablespoons butter or margarine
    1 package (⅝ oz.) Pillsbury Brown
      Gravy Mix or Home Style Gravy Mix

Preheat oven to 375°. Cut potatoes and carrots into 1-inch thick slices. Melt butter in 13x9-inch pan. Stir gravy mix into melted butter. Place vegetables in pan, rolling to coat well. Bake at 375°, turning once during baking, for 50 to 60 minutes until tender.   4 SERVINGS

Approximately 15 min.
SHERRIED CARROTS
    3 cups (6 med.) shredded carrots
    ½ teaspoon salt
    Dash pepper
    1 to 2 tablespoons brown sugar
    2 tablespoons butter or margarine
    ¼ cup cooking sherry

In medium saucepan, combine all ingredients. Cover and bring to a boil; simmer about 10 minutes until tender. If desired, garnish with chopped walnuts. Serve hot.   4 SERVINGS

Approximately 20 min.

QUICK ORANGEY CARROTS

- 5 medium carrots, cut in thin strips
- 2 tablespoons butter or margarine
- 2 tablespoons orange marmalade

Cook carrots in salted water for 15 to 20 minutes until tender; drain well. Add butter; cover and let stand a few minutes until butter melts. Stir in marmalade to glaze carrots. Serve immediately.   4 SERVINGS

One pan cooks both the croutons and the corn for this recipe — and saves you clean-up time.

Approximately 10 min.

CORN 'N CHEESEY CROUTONS

- ⅔ cup seasoned bread cubes
- 2 tablespoons grated Parmesan cheese
- 2 tablespoons butter or margarine
- 1¾ cups (17-oz. can) cream-style corn

In small saucepan, brown bread cubes and cheese in butter. Remove from pan and set aside. In same pan, heat corn on medium heat until heated through. To serve, garnish with browned bread cubes.   4 SERVINGS

Prepared chip dip that has been thinned with a little milk makes a very easy and ever-so-tasty sauce.

Pictured on page 43

Approximately 10 min.

CREAMY PEAS AND CORN

- 1½ cups (10-oz. pkg.) frozen corn
- 1½ cups (10-oz. pkg.) frozen peas
- ½ teaspoon salt
- ¼ cup prepared onion dip
- 1 tablespoon milk

Prepare peas and corn as directed on package. Drain well. Meanwhile, in small bowl, combine salt, dip and milk. Add to drained vegetables. Toss lightly to coat well. Serve hot.

6 TO 8 SERVINGS

Tip: If desired, 1½ cups (1-lb. can) peas and 1½ cups (1-lb. can) corn can be used for the frozen. Heat in liquid from can; drain well. Prepare as directed.

Quick Orangey Carrots

Put this dish together in no time at all. Your oven does the work after that — leaving you free to prepare the rest of your meal.

Approximately 50 min.

EGGPLANT PARMESAN

- ½ eggplant, peeled and sliced
- ½ teaspoon salt
- ¼ teaspoon Italian seasoning, if desired
- 1 cup (8-oz. can) spaghetti sauce
- ½ cup (2 oz.) grated Mozarella cheese
- 2 tablespoons grated Parmesan cheese

Preheat oven to 350°. Place eggplant slices in 1-quart casserole or baking dish. Sprinkle with salt and Italian seasoning. Top with spaghetti sauce and Mozarella cheese. Sprinkle Parmesan cheese over top. Bake, covered, at 350° for 20 minutes; uncover; continue baking 20 to 25 minutes until eggplant is tender and cheese is bubbly.   4 SERVINGS

Tip: If desired, oregano can be used for the Italian seasoning.

An easy-to-do, light-flavored deviled sauce gives a special flair to hominy.

Approximately 10 min.

CREAMY DEVILED HOMINY

2 cups (1 lb. 4-oz. can) drained hominy
1 tablespoon butter or margarine
½ cup dairy or imitation sour cream
½ teaspoon sugar
½ teaspoon chopped chives
½ teaspoon prepared mustard

In medium saucepan, heat drained hominy in butter, stirring frequently, until heated through. Remove from heat. Stir in remaining ingredients to coat well. Serve hot with salt and pepper, if desired.   4 SERVINGS

The dill from pickles provides the flavor for these peas. Adjust the sweetness to your own taste. Easy and very good.

Pictured on page 63
Approximately 10 min.

DILLY SWEET PEAS

1½ cups (10-oz. pkg.) frozen peas*
¼ cup (1 med.) chopped dill pickle
2 to 4 tablespoons butter or margarine
1 tablespoon dill pickle juice
1 to 2 teaspoons honey or sugar

Prepare peas as directed on package. Drain thoroughly. Toss with remaining ingredients. Serve hot.   4 SERVINGS

Tip:*If desired, 1½ cups (1-lb. can) drained peas can be used for the frozen.

Approximately 15 min.

ORANGE GLAZED PEAS

3 cups (two 10-oz. pkgs.) frozen peas*
½ teaspoon salt
⅛ teaspoon pepper
2 tablespoons butter or margarine
2 tablespoons orange marmalade

Cook peas as directed on package; drain well. Add remaining ingredients; toss lightly. Heat through. If desired, garnish with orange peel.   6 TO 8 SERVINGS

Tip:*If desired, canned peas can be used for the frozen peas.

Okra coated with crumbs and fried in butter or bacon drippings.

Pictured on page 21
Approximately 15 min.

SKILLET FRIED OKRA

1½ cups (10-oz. pkg.) frozen okra, partially thawed and cut into ½-inch pieces
2 tablespoons instant minced onion or ½ cup (1 small) chopped onion
⅓ cup cornmeal*
1 teaspoon salt
¼ teaspoon ground thyme, if desired
4 to 5 tablespoons butter or margarine

In medium mixing bowl, combine all ingredients except butter. In medium fry pan, melt butter. Add okra mixture. Cook over medium heat, stirring occasionally, until brown. Cover; reduce to low heat. Cook for about 5 minutes until tender. Serve immediately. 5 TO 6 SERVINGS

Tips:*Dry bread crumbs or cracker crumbs can be used for the cornmeal. Bacon drippings can be used for the butter.

Prepared cheese spreads make an easy, subtle-flavored sauce for vegetables. Use remainder of spread with crackers for quick appetizers.

Pictured on page 52
Approximately 10 min.

PIMIENTO CHEESE PEAS

1½ cups (10-oz. pkg.) frozen peas
2 tablespoons pimiento cheese spread

Cook peas as directed on package. Drain excess water. Add cheese spread to peas; let stand several minutes until heat from peas softens cheese. Stir lightly to mix well. Serve hot.   4 SERVINGS

Tips:Other flavors of cheese spread go well with peas. We particularly like smokey and blue cheese flavors.

If desired, 1 tablespoon chopped pimiento can be added to the peas without the cheese spread.

This cheese coating is good on either zucchini or eggplant (see Tip). Keep them hot and crisp in the oven if dinner is delayed.

Pictured on page 61
Approximately 20 min.
CHEESY FRIED ZUCCHINI
　¼ cup dry bread crumbs
　2 tablespoons grated Parmesan cheese
　2 tablespoons flour
　1 teaspoon salt
　2 cups (2 med.) thinly sliced zucchini
　　strips
　1 egg, beaten well
　2 to 4 tablespoons cooking oil

In shallow bowl or plastic bag, combine bread crumbs, Parmesan cheese, flour and salt; mix well. Dip zucchini strips in egg then in crumb mixture. Fry in hot oil on both sides until golden brown and crispy. Serve hot.

　　　　　　　　　　3 TO 4 SERVINGS

　　Tip: For Cheesy Fried Eggplant, use eggplant strips or slices for the zucchini.

A baked vegetable such as this one takes only a few minutes to put together. You're free while it bakes by itself.

Pictured on page 43
Approximately 1 hr.
SQUASH VERMONT
　3 acorn squash, halved
　½ teaspoon salt
　Dash pepper
　6 tablespoons butter or margarine
　6 tablespoons brown sugar
　6 slices bacon

Preheat oven to 400°. Place squash halves cut-side down on cookie sheet or pan. Bake at 400° for 45 to 50 minutes until tender. Meanwhile, fry bacon; drain on paper towel. Sprinkle each baked squash half with salt and pepper; dot with butter and top with brown sugar. Cut each slice of bacon into 3 pieces; lay the 3 pieces across each squash half. Bake at 400° for 10 to 12 minutes until bacon is brown.　　6 SERVINGS

　　Tip: If desired, 6 tablespoons maple-flavored syrup can be used for the butter and brown sugar, and Vienna sausages for the bacon. Prepare as directed.

Approximately 30 min.
CHEESY CRUMB TOMATOES
　6 tomatoes, halved
　½ cup bread crumbs
　2 tablespoons Parmesan cheese
　½ teaspoon salt
　⅛ teaspoon pepper
　2 tablespoons butter or margarine

Preheat oven to 400°. In small bowl, combine bread crumbs, cheese, salt and pepper; mix well. Sprinkle several tablespoons crumb mixture over each tomato half. Dot each half with 1 teaspoon butter (or drizzle with melted butter). Place on cookie sheet. Bake, uncovered, at 400° for 15 to 20 minutes. Serve hot.　　　　　　　　6 SERVINGS

Approximately 10 min.
PARMESAN BUTTERED SQUASH
　6 cups (about 2 lbs.) cubed or sliced
　　summer or zucchini squash*
　¼ cup water
　2 tablespoons butter or margarine
　½ teaspoon salt
　Dash pepper
　1 tablespoon grated Parmesan cheese

In medium saucepan, cook squash, covered, in water for 7 to 10 minutes, just until tender. Drain well. Add remaining ingredients. Toss lightly to mix well. Serve hot.　6 SERVINGS

An elegant French looking dish that is "today's woman" easy. Simple, yet exciting in flavor.

Approximately 15 min.
SPINACH ELEGANT
　1¾ cups (10-oz. pkg.) frozen spinach
　½ cup (4-oz. can) drained, sliced
　　mushrooms
　½ teaspoon salt
　½ teaspoon instant minced onion or
　　2 teaspoons chopped onion
　Dash pepper
　¼ cup dairy or imitation sour cream

Prepare spinach as directed on package, adding mushrooms, onion, salt and pepper with spinach; drain thoroughly. Stir in sour cream; mix lightly. Serve hot.　4 SERVINGS

Cheesy Crumb Tomatoes, opposite page

Gravy mix provides the base for this yummy sauce. Pineapple and vegetables look and taste delightfully interesting.
Pictured on page 81
Approximately 15 min.

SWEET-SOUR VEGETABLES

¾ cup (8-oz. can) pineapple chunks, drain and reserve ⅓ cup liquid

2 tablespoons vinegar

⅓ cup water

⅓ cup firmly packed brown sugar

Reserved ⅓ cup pineapple liquid

1 package (⅝ oz.) Pillsbury Home Style Gravy Mix

½ cup chopped green pepper

2 chopped green onions, if desired

1 carrot, cut into ⅛-inch slices

1 tomato, cut in thin wedges

2 tablespoons butter or margarine

Chow mein noodles

Drain pineapple, reserving juice. In medium saucepan, combine vinegar, water, brown sugar, pineapple juice and gravy mix. Cook, stirring occasionally, until thickened. In small fry pan, sauté pineapple and vegetables in butter until heated through. Add vegetables to sauce. Heat 3 minutes. Serve over heated chow mein noodles.   3 TO 4 SERVINGS

Create your own combination of vegetables and dry salad dressing mix with this recipe as a guide. Tasty and very quick.
Pictured on page 86
Approximately 10 min.

FRENCH SEASONED VEGETABLES

1¾ cups (10-oz. pkg.) frozen mixed vegetables

¼ to ½ teaspoon dry French salad dressing mix

Cook vegetables as directed on package. Drain; sprinkle salad dressing mix over vegetables. Allow to stand, covered, several minutes until flavors blend. Serve hot.

4 SERVINGS

Tips: Peas and carrots (or any combination of vegetables) can be used for the mixed vegetables.

Any of the dry salad dressing mixes can be used for the French. We especially like Italian and garlic cheese.

Approximately 10 min.

SHERRY GLAZED SWEETS

2 cups (18-oz. can) drained sweet potatoes or yams

¼ cup firmly packed brown sugar

2 tablespoons butter or margarine

2 tablespoons dry sherry

Preheat broiler. Place potatoes in small pan with sides for broiling. In small saucepan, combine butter and brown sugar. Heat, stirring occasionally, until butter is melted. Pour sugar mixture over potatoes. Drizzle with sherry. Broil 3 to 4 inches from heat for 5 to 8 minutes until potatoes are heated through and lightly browned on top. Spoon syrup mixture over potatoes to serve.   3 TO 4 SERVINGS

Pictured on page 86
Approximately 15 min.

MAPLE GLAZED SWEETS

3 cups (1 lb. 7-oz. can) drained sweet potatoes

½ teaspoon salt

¼ cup butter or margarine

½ cup maple-flavored syrup

½ teaspoon grated orange peel

In medium saucepan, combine all ingredients. Simmer, uncovered, over medium heat, occasionally stirring very gently, for 10 to 15 minutes. Syrup will thicken and glaze potatoes. Serve hot.   4 TO 6 SERVINGS

Beef bouillon and instant minced onion are the quick additions that make these potatoes "he-man" hearty.
Picture on page 27
Approximately 20 min.

HEARTY POTATOES

½ cup water

½ teaspoon salt

½ teaspoon instant minced onion

1 cube beef bouillon or 1 teaspoon instant bouillon

2 cups (3 med.) sliced or quartered potatoes

In large saucepan, bring water, salt, onion and beef bouillon to a boil. Add sliced potatoes; simmer, covered, 10 to 12 minutes for slices, 15 to 20 minutes for quarters, just until tender. Serve hot with butter or gravy. 3 TO 4 SERVINGS

Tip: Other types of bouillon (chicken, onion, vegetable) can be used for the beef.

Approximately 30 min.

DOUBLE TASTY POTATO FRY

    1 package (7¼ oz.) Pillsbury Hash Brown
        Potatoes
    1 package (⅝ oz.) Pillsbury Chicken
        Gravy Mix
    ½ cup butter or margarine

Simmer and drain potatoes as directed on
package. Melt butter in skillet; stir in gravy mix.
Add potatoes; fry until crisp and golden brown.
4 SERVINGS

*The flavor's terrific and easily accomplished
with a few common ingredients. A great meal
accompaniment.*

Pictured on page 16
Approximately 15 min.

'TATERS TERRIFIC

    ¼ cup (4 tablespoons) butter or margarine
    5 cups (16-oz. pkg.) frozen potato balls
    1 tablespoon parsley flakes
    2 teaspoons instant minced onion or
        3 tablespoons chopped onion
    Salt
    Pepper

In medium fry pan, melt butter. Add remaining
ingredients. Cook, stirring occasionally, over
medium high heat until potato balls are golden
brown and crispy. Serve hot. 4 TO 6 SERVINGS

*Small metal skewers speed the baking time for
potatoes by transferring heat to the center
more quickly.*

Pictured on page 32
Approximately 40 min.

SPEEDY BAKED POTATOES

Preheat oven to 325°. Scrub medium-sized
baking potatoes; wrap in foil if desired. Insert
metal skewers or fork tongs into center of
potatoes. Bake at 375° for 35 to 45 minutes
until tender. Serve with butter or Sour Cream
and Chive Topping, if desired.

Sour Cream and Chive Topping

    1 tablespoon chopped green onion or
        chopped chives
    ½ cup dairy or imitation sour cream

Combine all ingredients; mix well. Chill until
serving time.
½ CUP TOPPING

*Canned potatoes take the time consuming
pre-preparation out of this favorite. Cook them
whole, sliced or cubed.*

Pictured on page 72
Approximately 15 min.

QUICK POTATO BROWNS

    2 tablespoons butter or margarine
    2 cups (15-oz. can) drained small
        whole potatoes
    ½ teaspoon salt
    Dash pepper
    1 medium onion, sliced

In medium fry pan, brown potatoes in butter
over medium heat, seasoning with salt and
pepper during cooking. (Since canned potatoes
are already cooked, all they need is browning.)
Add onion near end of browning. Continue
cooking until tender. Serve hot.
3 TO 4 SERVINGS

Tips: If desired, garnish with chopped
parsley, dill weed or toasted sesame
seeds.
For Quick Home Fries or Hash Browns,
slice or chop potatoes before frying.

*This sweet-glazed potato and banana
combination is ready in a jiffy with the aid of
your broiler unit.*

Pictured on page 57
Approximately 15 min.

TROPICAL TATER BROIL

    2 cups (18-oz. can) drained sweet
        potatoes or yams
    2 bananas, peeled and cut into quarters
    ¼ cup firmly packed brown sugar
    ¼ cup corn syrup
    2 tablespoons butter or margarine

Preheat broiler. Arrange potatoes and bananas
in single layer in pan with sides for broiling.
In small saucepan, combine remaining
ingredients; heat, stirring occasionally, until
butter has melted. Pour syrup mixture over
potatoes and bananas; coating well. Broil 3 to
4 inches from heat for 5 to 8 minutes until
heated through and lightly brown on top. Spoon
syrup mixture over potatoes and bananas to
serve.
4 TO 5 SERVINGS

Rice, Noodles and Breads

RICE OR MASHED POTATO VARIATIONS

Prepare 4-serving recipe rice or Pillsbury Hungry Jack Mashed Potatoes as directed on package.

Stir in just until combined:
- ⅓ cup (3-oz. can) drained, broiled-in-butter sliced mushrooms

  OR
- ½ cup (4-oz. can) drained mushroom stems and pieces and 4 teaspoons chopped green onion sautéed in 1 tablespoon butter or margarine

  OR

Prepare 4-serving recipe rice or Pillsbury Hungry Jack Mashed Potatoes as directed on package adding to water:
- 1 tablespoon chopped parsley or parsley flakes
- 2 teaspoons chopped green onion
- ¼ teaspoon sweet basil

  OR

Prepare 4-serving recipe rice or Pillsbury Hungry Jack Mashed Potatoes as directed on package reducing water in potatoes to 1 cup.

Stir in just until combined a mixture of:
- ½ cup dairy or imitation sour cream
- ½ teaspoon garlic or cheese garlic or onion or blue cheese dry salad dressing mix

Grated Parmesan cheese and butter are easy but very tasty additions to this basic noodle dish.

Approximately 15 min.
NOODLES ALFREDO
- 2 cups (8 oz.) medium size egg noodles
- ½ cup butter or margarine, melted
- ½ cup grated Parmesan cheese

Cook noodles as directed on package until tender. Drain well. Add melted butter. Sprinkle on cheese and mix well. Serve immediately.

6 SERVINGS

RICE OR MASHED POTATO CASSEROLES
Stir in Seasonings:
Prepare 4-serving recipe of rice or Pillsbury Hungry Jack Mashed Potatoes as directed on package.

Stir in just until combined:
- ¼ cup grated Parmesan cheese
- ½ to ¾ teaspoon dill weed

  OR
- ½ cup blue cheese dip and
- ½ teaspoon MSG (monosodium glutamate), if desired

  OR
- 1 tablespoon each chopped chives and chopped parsley

Stir in Sour Cream and Herbs:
Prepare 4-serving recipe of rice or Pillsbury Hungry Jack Mashed Potatoes as directed on package reducing water in potatoes to 1 cup:

Stir in just until combined:
- ½ cup chive-onion dairy or imitation sour cream

  OR
- 1 teaspoon instant minced onion
- 2 tablespoons chopped parsley
- ⅛ teaspoon ground thyme and
- ½ cup dairy or imitation sour cream

  OR
- 2 tablespoons crumbled blue cheese
- ⅓ cup dairy or imitation sour cream

If desired, spoon into 1-quart round baking dish. Sprinkle with a mixture of 2 teaspoons butter or margarine, melted, and 2 tablespoons potato flakes. Bake at 400° for 10 minutes or broil for 4 to 5 minutes until flakes are brown.

Approximately 15 min.
RICE JARDINIÈRE
- 1 package (7 oz.) vegetables and rice mix
- 1 cup (8 oz. or ½ pt.) quartered cherry tomatoes

Prepare rice as directed on package. Add tomatoes during last 5 minutes of cooking. Stir very gently to mix together. Serve hot.

4 SERVINGS

Fold grated cheese into rice for a quick addition. The cheese melts to form small pockets of golden goodness.

Approximately 15 min.
POCKETS OF GOLD RICE

    4 servings (2 cups) cooked rice
    2 chicken bouillon cubes or 2 teaspoons
    instant bouillon
    ½ cup (2 oz.) grated Cheddar cheese

Prepare rice for 4 servings as directed on package, adding bouillon cubes to water. When rice is tender, gently stir in cheese. Place in serving dish. (Heat from the rice will melt the cheese.) Serve hot.   4 SERVINGS

    Tips: If desired, beef bouillon can be used for the chicken.
    Noodles can be used for the rice, if desired.

Approximately 15 min.
POPPY CHEESE NOODLES

    2 cups cooked noodles*
    ½ cup (2-oz.) grated American cheese
    ½ teaspoon poppy seeds

Prepare noodles as directed on package. Add cheese and poppy seeds to hot, prepared noodles. Cover; let stand 2 to 3 minutes. (Heat from noodles will melt cheese.) Serve hot.
                                4 SERVINGS

    Tip: *1½ cups uncooked noodles, prepared as directed on package, will give the 2 cups needed for this recipe.

Approximately 15 min.
RICE AND MUSHROOMS

    1 cup (8-oz. can) mushrooms, drain and
    reserve liquid
    1 beef bouillon cube or 1 teaspoon
    instant bouillon
    ¼ teaspoon salt
    2 cups quick-cooking rice

Drain mushrooms; reserve liquid. Add water to mushroom liquid to measure amount called for in package directions. Add mushrooms, beef bouillon cube and salt. Cook rice as directed on package.   4 SERVINGS

    Tip: If desired, 1 chicken bouillon cube can be used for the beef.

This is an especially good accompaniment for sweet-sour, curried and Oriental dishes, although it goes well with others as well. A fun variation for rice.

Pictured on page 44
Approximately 15 min.
QUICK ALMOND CURRANT RICE

    2 cups quick-cooking rice
    2 tablespoons butter or margarine
    ¼ teaspoon salt
    ¼ cup diced roasted almonds
    ¼ cup currants

Prepare rice as directed on package, adding butter and salt. Just before serving, stir in almonds and currants.   4 SERVINGS

    Tip: If desired, ¼ cup chopped almonds that have been browned in 1 tablespoon butter or margarine can be used for the diced roasted almonds.

This rice has a very hearty flavor and is sometimes served as a main dish when more meat is added. Great with Oriental dishes.

Pictured on page 81
Approximately 25 min.
QUICK FRIED RICE

    6 slices bacon
    1 tablespoon cooking oil
    1 onion, finely chopped
    2 eggs, slightly beaten
    4 cups cooked rice
    2 tablespoons soy sauce
    ½ teaspoon salt
    ½ teaspoon Worcestershire sauce
    ⅛ teaspoon pepper

In large fry pan, fry bacon until crisp. Drain on paper towel; crumble. Pour out bacon drippings. Heat oil in same fry pan. Fry onion and egg until cooked. Add bacon and remaining ingredients. Reduce heat. Cook over medium heat, stirring occasionally, for 10 to 15 minutes until mixture is heated through. Serve as an accompaniment to meat dishes.
                            4 TO 6 SERVINGS

A quick way to a breakfast, lunch or supper favorite — easy-to-do, too.

Approximately 15 min.
ENGLISH MUFFINS

Open 1 can (8 oz.) Pillsbury Refrigerated Biscuits; coat with cornmeal, if desired. Bake on moderately hot greased griddle (375°F.) or in covered greased fry pan until golden brown, about 5 minutes on each side.* Split and toast, brush with butter and serve hot.   10 MUFFINS

> Tip: *To make with electric skillet, preheat with dial set at 275°F. Brush skillet with butter or margarine. Open steam vents; bake in covered skillet for 10 minutes on each side.

Pictured on page 86
Approximately 20 min.
SPEEDY BREAD STICKS

> 1 can (8 oz.) Pillsbury Country Style or Buttermilk Refrigerated Biscuits
>
> 1 egg white, slightly beaten
>
> Coarse salt

Preheat oven to 400°. Cut each biscuit in half. Roll into pencil shape, about 4 to 6 inches long. Place on ungreased cookie sheet; brush with beaten egg white. Sprinkle with salt. Bake at 400° for 12 to 15 minutes until golden brown.
                    20 BREAD STICKS

> Tip: Use caraway, sesame or poppy seed or Parmesan cheese for the coarse salt, if desired.

Ready-to-bake biscuits are formed into loaves for this recipe. Very creative-looking.

Approximately 20 min.
CRUNCHY ONION MINI-LOAVES

> 1 can (8 oz.) Pillsbury Refrigerated Buttermilk Biscuits
>
> 1 tablespoon melted butter or margarine
>
> ¼ cup Pillsbury Hungry Jack Potato Flakes
>
> 1 teaspoon onion salt

Preheat oven to 375°. Form dough into 2 loaves. Brush with melted butter. In shallow bowl, combine potato flakes and onion salt. Roll loaves in potato mixture. Place each loaf 5 to 6 inches apart on ungreased cookie sheet. Bake at 375° for 15 to 18 minutes until golden brown. Serve warm.   TWO 7-INCH LOAVES

Create your own unique dinner rolls with the following suggested variations or some of your own ideas.

Approximately 15 min.
VARIETY DINNER ROLL BASKET

Preheat oven to 375°. Separate dough from one can (8 oz.) Pillsbury Refrigerated Quick Crescent Dinner Rolls into 8 triangles. Brush each with melted butter or lightly spread with cream cheese. Sprinkle with one or more of the following:

garlic powder or salt	dill seed
onion powder or salt	chopped peanuts
poultry seasoning	candied fruit
chives	Parmesan cheese
caraway seed	lemon pepper marinade
sesame seed	parsley
poppy seed	shredded Cheddar cheese

Or, separate the dough into triangles and lightly spread each with one of the following:

honey	preserves
apple butter	mincemeat
barbecue sauce	

Roll up, starting with wide end. Place on ungreased cookie sheet. If desired, brush with butter and sprinkle tops with more of one of the variations. Bake at 375° for 10 to 12 minutes until golden brown. Serve warm.   8 ROLLS

A quick dip in prepared barbecue sauce gives these rolls a creative touch. Very easy!

Approximately 15 min.

CHEESY BARBECUE ROLLS

1 can (8-oz.) Pillsbury Refrigerated Butterflake Dinner Rolls

2 tablespoons prepared barbecue sauce

¼ cup grated Parmesan cheese

Preheat oven to 375°. Stand 2 rolls on edge in each greased muffin cup. Dip rolls in barbecue sauce then in cheese. Bake at 375° for 12 to 15 minutes or until golden brown. Serve warm.

6 ROLLS

Approximately 15 min.

BUTTERFLAKE HERB ROLLS

1 can (8 oz.) Pillsbury Refrigerated Quick Butterflake Dinner Rolls

2 tablespoons butter or margarine, melted

2 tablespoons chopped parsley or parsley flakes or ½ teaspoon caraway or poppy seed

Preheat oven to 375°. Place rolls in greased muffin pans as directed on label. Brush with melted butter; sprinkle with parsley and/or seeds. Bake at 375° for 12 to 14 minutes until golden brown. Serve warm.

12 SMALL OR 6 DOUBLE ROLLS

Butterflake Herb Rolls, above

Fun additions to refrigerated dough, plus a new shape, make this a tasty and clever-looking bread.

Pictured on page 49

Approximately 30 min.

CONFETTI CHEESE BREAD

2 tablespoons butter or margarine

⅓ cup shredded Cheddar cheese

¼ cup chopped green pepper

2 tablespoons bacon bits, if desired

2 tablespoons chopped pimiento

1 teaspoon instant minced onion

1 can (8 oz.) Pillsbury Refrigerated Buttermilk or Country Style Biscuits

Preheat oven to 400°. In a medium size saucepan, melt butter. Add cheese, pepper, bacon bits, pimiento and onion. Separate dough into 10 biscuits and cut each biscuit into 4 pieces. Drop a few biscuit quarters at a time into the cheese mixture while tossing lightly with forks. Turn into a well greased 8-inch round pan; distribute evenly. Bake at 400° for 18 to 20 minutes until golden brown. Cool 5 minutes before removing from pan. Serve warm or cold.

1 ROUND LOAF (6 SERVINGS)

Use prepared corn bread mix as a convenient base for muffins, corn bread or fritters.

Approximately 30 min.

CORNY CORN BREAD MUFFINS

1 package (8½ oz.) corn bread muffin mix

1 cup (8-oz. can) drained whole kernel corn*

Preheat oven to 400°. Prepare corn bread muffin mix as directed on package, adding corn to batter before placing in muffin cups. Fill greased or paper-lined muffin cups ½ to ⅔ full. Bake at 400° for 15 to 20 minutes until light golden brown. Serve hot with butter.

8 TO 10 MUFFINS

Tip: *For Mexi-Corn Bread Muffins, corn with red and green peppers can be used for the regular.

Desserts

Saucy Apple Swirl Cake, page 120, Spicy Apple Crescents, page 123, Mandarin Orange Whip, page 111 and Mocha Pie, page 123.

A prepared drink mix adds a sensational flavor to this pudding dessert. Let it chill while you're eating dinner for a great finalé.

Pictured on page 27
Approximately 30 min.
EGGNOG BAVARIAN

   1 package (3¾ oz.) instant vanilla
      pudding mix
  1½ cups milk
   ¼ cup eggnog flavored beads
   1 cup frozen prepared whipped topping,
      thawed

Prepare vanilla pudding as directed on package, decreasing milk to 1½ cups and adding eggnog beads. When mixture thickens, fold in whipped topping. Pour into individual serving dishes. If desired, garnish with a sprinkle of ground nutmeg. Chill 15 minutes or until serving time.   4 SERVINGS

Approximately 50 min.
EASY PEACH CLOUDS

   2 cups (16-oz. can) peach pie filling
   1 tablespoon apricot or peach brandy
   ⅛ teaspoon almond extract, if desired
   2 cups (1 pt.) frozen whipped topping

In medium mixing bowl, beat pie filling on low speed until peaches are in small pieces. Mix in brandy and almond extract. Fold in whipped topping. Garnish with maraschino cherries, ground nutmeg or toasted coconut. Spoon into individual serving bowls; place in freezer for 30 to 45 minutes until serving time.
    4 SERVINGS

Approximately 45 min.
MANDARIN ORANGE WHIP

   2 cups (1 pt.) prepared whipped topping
   1 cup (8-oz. carton) orange flavored
      yogurt
  1⅓ cups (11-oz. can) drained mandarin
      orange sections

In medium mixing bowl, add yogurt to whipped topping, stirring gently to combine. Fold in orange sections. Spoon into serving bowl or individual serving dishes; garnish with crumbled macaroons, cookie crumbs or chopped nuts. Chill in freezer for 30 minutes until serving time.
    5 TO 6 SERVINGS

Grasshopper pie appears as a pudding in this quick dessert. Elegant flavors and attractive colors.

Pictured on cover
Approximately 40 min.
LAZY GRASSHOPPER DESSERT PUDDING

   ⅔ cup crushed chocolate wafers
   2 cups (1 pt.) vanilla frozen pudding
      dessert, thawed*
   2 tablespoons creme de menthe
   1 tablespoon creme de cacao

Spread ⅓ cup of the chocolate wafers evenly over bottom of 1-quart dish. Reserve remaining crumbs for topping. In small mixing bowl, combine remaining ingredients; fold gently but thoroughly. Spoon pudding on top of crumbs; top with remaining ⅓ cup crumbs. Chill in freezer for 30 minutes or until serving time.
    4 SERVINGS

Tip: *If desired, 1 package (3¾ oz.) vanilla instant pudding mix, prepared as directed on package, can be used for the frozen pudding.

A shortcutted way to a banana cream favorite. Flavors mellow as they chill in the refrigerator.

Approximately 50 min.
BANANA CREAM PUDDING PIE

   2 cups (18-oz. can) prepared vanilla
      pudding
   2 bananas, sliced
   2 cups vanilla wafers

Line 9-inch pie pan or 9x5-inch loaf pan with half of vanilla wafers. Top with half of banana slices. Spoon 1 cup of the pudding on top. Repeat layering, ending with pudding. If desired, garnish with whipped topping or shredded coconut. Place in refrigerator for 30 to 45 minutes until ready to serve. Spoon to serve.   4 SERVINGS

Tips: Instant vanilla pudding mix can be used for the prepared pudding. Prepare as directed on package.

Banana Cream Pudding Pie can be prepared in individual serving dishes. Layer as directed.

For Snappy Apricot Pudding Pie, use gingersnaps for the vanilla wafers and drained apricot halves for the bananas.

Approximately 20 min.

VANUTTA PUDDING

- 1 package (3¾ oz.) instant vanilla pudding mix
- 1¾ cups cold milk
- ½ cup chunky or creamy peanut butter

Prepare pudding as directed on package, adding only 1¾ cups milk. When mixture has started to thicken, stir in peanut butter until well blended. Spoon into serving dishes. Garnish with chocolate curls, chocolate chips or chopped peanuts. Chill until ready to serve.

4 SERVINGS

Tip: Butterscotch or chocolate pudding mix can be used for the vanilla.

Approximately 20 min.

CHOCO MINT PUDDING

- 2 cups (1-pt. container) frozen prepared chocolate pudding
- ½ cup crushed peppermint candies

Thaw pudding as directed on package. Reserve 1 tablespoon crushed candy for garnish. Fold remainder of candy into pudding. Pour into serving dish or individual bowls. Garnish with reserved candy. Serve immediately or chill until serving time.

4 SERVINGS

Approximately 5 min.

CHOCOLATE MOCHA FRAPPÉ

- 2 cups (1 pt.) chocolate ice cream
- ¼ cup milk
- ¼ cup creme de cacao
- ¼ teaspoon instant coffee

Combine all ingredients in blender. Process for 30 seconds on highest speed. Pour into glasses.

2 SERVINGS

Tips: For Creme de Menthe Frappé, use vanilla ice cream and creme de menthe for the chocolate and creme de cacao; omit coffee. Prepare as directed.

Other combinations of ice cream and liqueur which we like are:

Chocolate ice cream and creme de menthe.

Strawberry ice cream and apricot or peach brandy.

Lime sherbet and creme de cacao.

Vanilla ice cream, light rum and 1 packet daiquiri mix.

A lovely dessert that takes a minimum of time to assemble. Refreshing and light.

Approximately 35 min.

LIGHT AND LAZY MINT WHIP

- 8 lady fingers, cut into thirds*
- 2 cups (1 pt.) frozen prepared whipped topping, thawed**
- 1 cup colored dinner mints

In medium mixing bowl, combine all ingredients; stir to mix well. Spoon into 8x4 or 9x5-inch loaf pan. Chill in freezer for 30 minutes until ready to serve. Cut in squares or spoon into individual dishes.

4 TO 6 SERVINGS

Tips: *Leftover cake cubes can be used for the lady fingers. Prepare as directed.

**If desired, 1 envelope (2 oz.) whipped topping mix, prepared as directed on package, can be used for the frozen.

Instant pudding is used for the flavor in these quick and easy bar or dessert squares. Pick a pudding with the flavor of cookie you want.

Approximately 50 min.

PICK A PUDDING TREATS

- ½ cup butter or margarine, softened
- 1 package (4 oz.) instant pudding mix, any flavor
- 2 eggs
- 1 teaspoon vanilla
- ¾ cup Pillsbury All Purpose Flour*
- ¾ teaspoon baking powder
- ½ to 1 cup chopped nuts

Preheat oven to 350°. In medium mixing bowl, cream butter; blend in instant pudding mix. Beat in eggs and vanilla. Add flour and baking powder; mix thoroughly. Stir in nuts. Spread in greased 8-inch square or round layer pan. Bake at 350° for 20 to 25 minutes until bars feel firm to the touch. Cool; cut into small bars or into dessert squares and serve with ice cream or whipped cream.

18 BAR COOKIES OR
9 DESSERT SERVINGS

Tips: With vanilla pudding, substitute ½ cup raisins for half of the nuts.

Or, with coconut pudding, sprinkle ½ cup flaked coconut over the top before baking.

*For use with Pillsbury Self-Rising Flour, omit baking powder.

Approximately 20 min.
BANANA PUDDING SPLIT

    1 package (3¾ oz.) instant vanilla or chocolate pudding mix

    2 bananas, halved

    Ice cream toppings, if desired

Prepare pudding as directed on package. Split banana halves in half lengthwise. Place two banana quarters in each serving dish. Spoon pudding over bananas. If desired, garnish with fudge sauce, your favorite ice cream topping, chopped nuts or sweetened whipped cream.

                4 SERVINGS

A very refreshing and light dessert! Perfect for topping off a delicious dinner.

Approximately 30 min.
DAIQUIRI PEACHES

    1 packet (1 oz.) frozen daiquiri mix

    2 to 3 peaches, peeled and sliced*

    1 tablespoon sugar

    ¼ teaspoon rum extract or 2 tablespoons light rum

Combine all ingredients. Mix to coat well. Chill 20 minutes or until ready to serve. If desired, garnish with lime slices.   2 TO 3 SERVINGS

    Tip: If desired, 2 cups (1 lb. 13-oz. can) drained peach halves or slices can be used for the fresh.

Approximately 30 min.
PEACH COBBLER

    1 can (8 oz.) Pillsbury Refrigerated Biscuits

    2 cups (1-lb. can) peach pie filling

    2 tablespoons melted butter or margarine

    Cinnamon-sugar

Preheat oven to 425°. Pour pie filling into a 1½-quart shallow casserole or 8-inch square pan. Cut biscuits in half, making half circles; dip in melted butter, then cinnamon-sugar. Place on top of peach filling. Bake at 425° for 15 to 20 minutes until biscuits are golden brown. Serve warm with ice cream or whipped cream.   5 TO 6 SERVINGS

    Tip: Other flavors prepared pie filling can be used for a variety of cobblers.

This fruit dessert goes together in a jiffy. A nice combination of flavors for a light dessert.

Approximately 35 min.
ORANGE-RUM BAKED BANANAS

    2½ cups (2 large) sliced bananas

    1½ cups (2 med.) peeled and sectioned oranges*

    3 tablespoons brown sugar

    3 tablespoons rum

    ½ cup whipped topping or sweetened whipped cream

Preheat oven to 300°. Place banana slices in bottom of 8x8-inch baking pan or 1-quart casserole; top with orange sections. Sprinkle sugar over fruit. Bake at 300° for 20 to 25 minutes until hot and bubbly. Mix rum with whipped topping. Serve fruit hot, topped with whipped topping mixture.   4 SERVINGS

    Tip: *If desired, canned orange sections can be used for the fresh.

Your favorite combination of mixed fruits is baked in a yummy coconut mixture. Delicious served with ice cream!

Approximately 45 min.
BAKED FRUIT AMBROSIA

    2 tablespoons butter or margarine

    ½ to ¾ cup grated or flaked coconut

    ¼ cup flour

    ⅓ cup firmly packed brown sugar

    ½ teaspoon salt

    2 cups (1 lb. 4-oz. can) drained pineapple chunks or tidbits

    2 cups (1 lb. 13-oz. can) drained sliced peaches

    1¾ cups (1-lb. can) drained pitted dark cherries

Preheat oven to 400°. While preheating oven, melt butter in 1½-quart casserole; remove from oven. Stir in coconut, flour, brown sugar and salt; mix thoroughly with fork. Add fruits; toss very lightly. Bake, uncovered, at 400° for 30 to 35 minutes until hot and bubbly. Serve warm.   4 TO 5 SERVINGS

    Tip: Other fruits can be substituted for the ones listed above as desired.

Bananas served in a flaming brandy sauce over ice cream. What could be more elegant!

Approximately 10 min.
BANANAS ROYALE
     4 medium bananas, peeled
     ⅓ cup butter or margarine
     ⅓ cup firmly packed brown sugar
     ¼ teaspoon cinnamon
     ¼ teaspoon ground nutmeg
     ¼ cup light cream
     ¼ to ⅓ cup brandy*
     4 cups (2 pts.) vanilla ice cream

Slice bananas in half, then lengthwise. In chafing dish or fondue pot, melt butter. Stir in brown sugar, cinnamon and nutmeg. Add bananas; cook 3 to 4 minutes. Stir in cream, cooking until thickened, about 2 minutes. Just before serving, heat brandy in small saucepan or ladle; ignite. Quickly pour over bananas in chafing dish. Serve flaming over ice cream.
6 TO 8 SERVINGS

Tips: *Or use 2 teaspoons brandy or rum flavoring, adding to sauce with cream. Serve hot over ice cream.

Recipe can be halved. Use 3 tablespoons each of butter, brown sugar and brandy.

If chafing dish is not available, a large heavy saucepan or double boiler will work satisfactorily.

Very easy to put together. Start them before you fix dinner and let them bake by themselves.
Pictured on page 52
Approximately 60 min.
CINNAMON APPLE BAKE
     6 baking apples, cored
     1 cup firmly packed brown sugar
     3 to 6 tablespoons butter or margarine
     6 tablespoons cinnamon candies
     ¾ cup water

Preheat oven to 375°. Remove peel around top of cored apples. Place in baking dish. Fill each center with 2 to 3 tablespoons brown sugar and 1 tablespoon cinnamon candies. Top each with ½ tablespoon butter. Pour water around apples. Bake at 375° for 45 to 60 minutes until apples are tender.   6 SERVINGS

Pictured on page 16
Approximately 15 min.
CINNAMON CANDY PEACHES
     3½ cups (1 lb. 13-oz. can) undrained peach halves or slices
     ¼ cup cinnamon candies
     1 tablespoon cornstarch
     ½ teaspoon whole cloves or ⅛ teaspoon ground cloves

In medium saucepan, combine liquid from peaches with cinnamon candies, cornstarch and cloves. Bring to a gentle boil and simmer until candies have melted. Remove whole cloves. Pour syrup over peaches. Serve warm or chilled. If desired, garnish with whipped topping.   4 TO 5 SERVINGS

Approximately 25 min.
SHERRY BROILED GRAPEFRUIT
     3 grapefruit
     6 tablespoons brown sugar
     6 tablespoons sherry or brandy
     6 tablespoons butter or margarine

Halve grapefruit. Top each half with 1 tablespoon each of brown sugar, sherry and butter. Let stand 15 minutes or while broiler heats. Broil 3 to 4 inches from heat for 5 to 8 minutes until lightly browned and bubbly on top.
6 SERVINGS

Tip: Granulated white sugar can be used for the brown sugar.

Approximately 15 min.
TOASTED COCONUT SUNDAE SQUARES
     1 package (14 oz.) Pillsbury Refrigerated Turnover Pastries
     ½ cup flaked coconut
     2 cups (1 pt.) any flavor ice cream

Preheat oven to 400°. Unroll and separate dough into 8 squares; place on ungreased cookie sheet. Squeeze icing from turnover package on each square; spread. Sprinkle about 1 tablespoon coconut on each square. Bake at 400° for 9 to 11 minutes, until golden brown. Before serving, place a scoop of ice cream on each square; top with about 1 tablespoon fruit filling.   8 SUNDAES

Approximately 15 min.
FRUIT FONDUE AU RUM

- 3 cups firmly packed brown sugar
- 1 cup light cream or evaporated milk
- ⅓ cup butter or margarine
- ¼ cup rum or 2 teaspoons rum flavoring
- Assorted fresh frozen or canned fruits, well drained and cut into 1-inch pieces*
- Pecan or walnut halves

In medium saucepan, combine brown sugar, cream and butter. Cook over medium heat, stirring constantly, until mixture begins to boil; boil for 3 minutes until sauce thickens. Remove from heat. Let stand about 3 minutes; stir in rum. Serve warm or cold by spearing fruits and nuts with fork and dipping into rum sauce. ABOUT 2 CUPS SAUCE (8 TO 10 SERVINGS)

Tips: *Orange or tangarine sections, pineapple chunks, strawberries, apple or pear pieces, mandarin oranges, bananas or cherries can be used for dipping in fondue. Squares of angelfood or sponge cake and large marshmallows can also be used for dipping.

Best if served in a dish that can be kept warm at the table. If pottery serving dish is unavailable, serve in individual cups.

To make ahead, prepare, cover and refrigerate. Or, prepare sauce except for adding rum. Just before serving, reheat and let stand for 3 minutes; stir in rum.

This makes an excellent sauce for serving with ice cream and other desserts.

Approximately 5 min.
MINT WHIP PEACHES

- 2 to 4 tablespoons creme de menthe or other liqueur
- 1 to 1½ cups prepared whipped topping
- 2 cups (1 lb. 13-oz. can) well-drained peach slices

In medium mixing bowl, combine liqueur and whipped topping; stir to blend well. Add peach slices. Stir gently to coat well. Serve in individual bowls. If desired, garnish with mint leaves or maraschino cherries.
6 TO 8 SERVINGS

Fruit Fondue au Rum

Approximately 25 min.
HONEY LIME MELON BALLS

    3 to 4 cups (1 med. or 1 large)
        canteloupe balls*
    1 to 2 tablespoons honey
    1 lime, sliced

In medium bowl, combine all ingredients. Chill in refrigerator 15 minutes or until ready to serve. Garnish with grated coconut or lime peel.
                                    4 SERVINGS

    Tips: *Other melons can be used for the canteloupe.
    For easy preparation, cut melon into bite-sized chunks instead of melon balls.
    Frozen melon balls can be used for the fresh.
    Lemon slices can be used for the lime.

With ingredients you have on hand, you can be ready with this dessert at the drop of a hat. It's fun for kids to make, too!

Approximately 1 hr.
APPLEMALLOW BAKE

    6 cups (6 med.) peeled and thinly sliced
        apples
    ¼ cup cinnamon candies
    3 cups miniature marshmallows

Preheat oven to 350°. In ungreased 9x5-inch loaf pan or 1-quart baking dish, mix apples, cinnamon candies and 2 cups of the marshmallows. Top with remaining 1 cup marshmallows. Bake, uncovered, at 350° for 45 to 50 minutes until apples are tender. Serve hot.   6 SERVINGS

Approximately 10 min.
STRAWBERRIES DELUXE

    ½ cup dairy sour cream
    ¼ cup firmly packed brown sugar
    1 pint (2 cups) whole strawberries,
        hulled

In medium bowl, combine sour cream and brown sugar. Add strawberries; toss lightly to coat well. Serve chilled in individual dishes alone or as a topping for a shortcake or dessert waffle.   4 SERVINGS

    Tip: Other fruits can be used for the strawberries. Choose your favorite.

Easy-Cheesy Lemon Bars,

These bars taste much like lemon cheesecake. Make them before you start fixing dinner so they'll have a chance to cool by the time you're ready for dessert.

Approximately 1 hr.
EASY-CHEESY LEMON BARS

    1 package Pillsbury Lemon Cake Mix
    ½ cup butter or margarine, melted
    1 egg
    1 package Pillsbury Buttercream Lemon
        Frosting Mix
    1 package (8 oz.) cream cheese, softened
    2 eggs

Preheat oven to 350°. Combine cake mix, butter and 1 egg. Stir until moist. Pat into 13x9-inch pan, greased on bottom only. Blend frosting mix into softened cream cheese. Reserve ½ cup for frosting baked bars. Add 2 eggs to remaining frosting mixture. Beat 3 to 5 minutes. Spread over base. Bake at 350° for 30 to 40 minutes. Cool; frost with reserved frosting.   13x9-INCH PAN

HIGH ALTITUDE ADJUSTMENT — 5,200 feet. Bake at 375°.

Approximately 25 min.

QUICK COCONUT DELIGHTS

- 1 package Pillsbury Fluffy White Frosting Mix
- ⅓ cup boiling water
- ½ cup flour
- 1 cup flaked or shredded coconut
- 1 teaspoon almond extract

Preheat oven to 325°. Prepare frosting mix using ⅓ cup boiling water; blend thoroughly and beat at highest speed until stiff peaks form that bend slightly. Fold in flour, coconut and almond extract. Drop by teaspoonfuls onto lightly greased cookie sheet. Bake at 325° for 10 to 12 minutes. Do not overbake. Remove from cookie sheet immediately. Store in covered container.

ABOUT 3½ DOZEN COOKIES

These holiday looking cookies are made in half the time by using refrigerated cookie dough. So easy kids can make them, too.

Approximately 20 min.

JEWELED THUMBPRINTS

- 1 roll (18 oz.) Pillsbury Refrigerated Sugar Slice 'N Bake Cookies
- ¼ cup melted butter or margarine
- 2 cups chopped pecans
- Red or green jelly

Preheat oven to 375°. Slice cookie dough ¾-inch thick and cut each slice into four quarters. Roll each into a ball. Dip in butter; roll in nuts. Place on ungreased cookie sheet. Bake at 375° for 10 to 12 minutes until golden brown. Remove from oven; quickly indent the center of each with finger. Place ¼ to ½ teaspoon jelly in each center. Cool.

48 COOKIES

Jeweled Thumbprints, above

Use a common ingredient — pancake mix — to make butterscotch flavored bars. Good as a dessert or as a snack.

Approximately 1 hr.

SNAPPY JACKS

- ⅔ cup shortening
- ⅔ cup sugar
- 2 eggs
- 2 cups Pillsbury Hungry Jack Buttermilk Pancake Mix
- 2 teaspoons ground allspice
- 1 cup (6 oz.) butterscotch pieces
- 1 cup chopped walnuts

Preheat oven to 350°. Cream shortening and sugar until well blended and fluffy. Beat in eggs. Add dry pancake mix, allspice, butterscotch pieces and nuts; mix well. Spread in generously greased 13x9-inch square pan. Bake at 350° for 25 to 30 minutes, or until golden brown. Cool. Frost and cut into bars.

Frosting: Prepare 1 small package Pillsbury Vanilla Frosting Mix as directed on package.

24 BARS

Approximately 20 min.

DO-LITTLE CHOCOLATE MACAROONS

- ½ cup Pillsbury All Purpose or Self-Rising Flour
- 1 package (4½ oz.) instant chocolate pudding mix
- 2 cups flaked coconut
- 1 cup sweetened condensed milk
- ½ teaspoon almond extract

Preheat oven to 325°. In large mixing bowl, combine all ingredients; mix well. Drop by teaspoons, 2 inches apart, onto greased and floured cookie sheets. Bake at 325° for 10 to 12 minutes until cookie is firm. Carefully remove from cookie sheets immediately.

ABOUT 30 COOKIES

Tip: Try with instant butterscotch or lemon pudding mix for butterscotch or lemon macaroons; use vanilla for almond extract.

Make this delightful Danish pastry in less than a half an hour with refrigerated dough. Great for dessert, brunch or breakfast.

Approximately 25 min.
ALMOND BEAR CLAWS
  ⅔ cup powdered sugar
  ½ cup (4 oz.) almond paste
  1 egg, slightly beaten
  Dash salt
  1 can (8 oz.) Pillsbury Refrigerated Quick Crescent Dinner Rolls
  2 to 4 tablespoons powdered sugar
  2 tablespoons sliced almonds

Preheat oven to 375°. Combine ⅔ cup powdered sugar, almond paste, 2 tablespoons beaten egg (reserve remaining egg for glaze) and salt; beat until smooth. Unroll crescent dough to form two 13x4-inch rectangles. Press perforations to seal. Spread almond mixture LENGTHWISE down center third of rectangles. Fold uncovered dough over almond mixture. Cut each strip into 4 pieces; place on greased cookie sheet, seam-side down. Brush surface with remaining egg and sprinkle with 2 to 4 tablespoons powdered sugar. On each piece, cut 4 slashes from one folded edge to center; bend dough slightly to separate slashes. Sprinkle tops with almonds. Bake at 375° for 12 to 15 minutes until golden. Serve warm or cold.   8 PASTRIES

Tips: If desired, ½ cup of your favorite cake and pastry filling can be used for almond filling.

To make ahead, prepare, cover and refrigerate up to 2 hours. Bake as directed.

Reheat, loosely wrapped in foil, at 325° for 10 to 15 minutes until heated through.

Approximately 25 min.
CINNAMON FLYING SAUCERS
  ¼ cup sugar
  ½ to 1 teaspoon cinnamon
  1 can (11.7 oz.) Pillsbury Refrigerated Quick Cinnamon Danish Rolls with Raisins
  2 tablespoons melted butter or margarine
  ¼ cup chopped walnuts

Preheat oven to 375°. Combine sugar and cinnamon. Separate dough into 8 rolls; brush with butter. Dip rolls in sugar mixture; place on lightly greased cookie sheet 3 inches apart. Press each to form a 4-inch circle. Bake at 375° for 12 to 14 minutes until golden brown. Spread with icing; sprinkle with nuts. 8 ROLLS

Approximately 30 min.

COCONUT HONEY CINNAMON ROLLS

    1 can (9.5 oz.) Pillsbury Quick Cinnamon
      Rolls with Icing
    2 tablespoons honey
    1 tablespoon melted butter or margarine
    ½ cup coconut

Preheat oven to 375°. Butter or grease cake pan. Open can and separate rolls. Mix honey and butter in small bowl. Dip cinnamon side of each roll in honey-butter mixture, then dip in coconut. Place rolls in 8-inch cake pan, cinnamon-side up. Bake at 375° for 18 to 22 minutes until golden brown. Spread with icing. Serve warm.   8 ROLLS

Approximately 40 min.

MINCEMEAT ICE CREAM

    2 cups (1 pt.) vanilla ice cream
    ¼ cup prepared mincemeat
    2 tablespoons sherry, rum or brandy

Soften ice cream slightly with back of spoon. (Do not over soften. Very soft ice cream requires longer freezing time to harden.) Fold in mincemeat and sherry. Spoon into ice cube tray or individual molds. Harden in freezer for 30 minutes or until serving time. Serve plain or with additional sherry spooned over.

                                4 SERVINGS

Crisp rice cereal forms the crust for this fun ice cream dessert — a pleaser for children, as well as adults.

Approximately 1 hr.

BUTTERSCOTCH PECAN FREEZE

    3 tablespoons butter or margarine
    1 package (6 oz.) butterscotch pieces
    3 cups crispy rice cereal
    2 pints butter pecan, butter brickle or
      chocolate ice cream

Put ice cream out at room temperature to soften while preparing crust. In large saucepan melt butter and butterscotch pieces over very low heat. Combine with cereal. Pat into 8x8-inch pan. Spoon in ice cream. Place in freezer about 30 to 45 minutes until ice cream is hard. Cut into squares or slices to serve.

                            6 TO 8 SERVINGS

    Tip: Chocolate, lemon or cherry chips can
    be used for the butterscotch. Combine
    them with your favorite flavor of ice cream.

Approximately 20 min.

DOUBLE DELIGHT FRUIT CUP

    1 package (14 oz.) Pillsbury Refrigerated
      Turnover Pastries
    1⅓ cups (1-lb. can) drained peach slices
    2 cups (1 pt.) any flavor ice cream

Preheat oven to 400°. Unroll and separate dough into 8 squares; gently press each square into ungreased muffin cups, allowing 4 corners of squares to extend over edge of cups. Pinch each corner to form points. Place two peach slices in each cup. Bake at 400° for 9 to 11 minutes until golden brown. Before serving, place a scoop of ice cream on each tart; top with about 1 tablespoon fruit filling combined with icing from turnover package.

                                8 SERVINGS

    Tips: Other drained, cooked fruit may be
    substituted for the peach slices such as
    apricot halves, apple slices or pineapple
    chunks.
    Dough squares can be baked on an
    ungreased cookie sheet; place three
    peach slices pinwheel fashion on squares
    before baking. Continue as directed.

Pictured on page 63

Approximately 5 min.

MINTY FRUIT ICE

    4 slices pineapple
    1 pint (2 cups) lemon sherbet
    ¼ cup mint jelly

Place pineapple slice or ring in individual bowls or dishes. Top with ½ cup sherbet and 1 tablespoon jelly. Serve cold. If desired, garnish with mint leaf.   4 SERVINGS

    Tip: Other flavors of sherbet can be used.
    We particularly like lime and raspberry.

Approximately 45 min.

PEACH GLORY COFFEE CAKE

    1 package (14 oz.) Pillsbury Butter Pecan
      Coffee Cake Mix
    1½ cups (12-oz. pkg.) frozen peach slices,
      thawed and drained

Preheat oven to 350°. Prepare and bake coffee cake as directed on package. Arrange peach slices on baked coffee cake. Spoon remaining topping over peaches.

                    8-INCH ROUND COFFEE CAKE

Custard mix adds a delicate richness to this Bundt cake. Its uses are as versatile as a pound cake or shortcake.

Approximately 1 hr.

EGG CUSTARD CAKE

½ cup (3-oz. pkg.) egg custard mix

1½ cups milk

2 eggs

1 package Pillsbury Yellow Cake Mix

Preheat oven to 350°. Generously grease and lightly flour bottom and sides of 10-inch Bundt or tube pan. In large mixer bowl, combine egg custard mix, milk and eggs. Blend at low speed until smooth. Add cake mix; blend and beat as directed on package. Pour into prepared pan. Bake at 350° for 40 to 45 minutes or until cake springs back when touched lightly in center. Cool cake 15 minutes before removing from pan. Serve plain or as a shortcake base, or spread with butter or margarine, sprinkle with a cinnamon-sugar mixture and toast in the oven.

10-INCH BUNDT OR TUBE CAKE

HIGH ALTITUDE ADJUSTMENT — 5,200 feet. Bake at 375° for 35 to 40 minutes.

Pictured on page 110
Approximately 1 hr.

SAUCY APPLE SWIRL CAKE

¼ cup sugar

2 teaspoons cinnamon

1 package (17 oz.) Pillsbury Yellow Cake Mix

1⅔ cups (1-lb. jar) applesauce

3 eggs

Preheat oven to 350°. Blend sugar and cinnamon. Grease 10-inch Bundt or tube pan and dust with about 1 tablespoon of sugar-cinnamon mixture; save remainder for cake. Blend cake mix, applesauce and eggs until moistened. Beat as directed on package. Reserve 1½ cups batter. Pour remaining batter into pan. Sprinkle with remaining sugar-cinnamon mixture; then top with reserved batter. Bake at 350° for 35 to 45 minutes or until done. Cool cake in pan, top-side up, for 15 minutes. Then invert on serving plate.

10-INCH BUNDT OR TUBE CAKE

HIGH ALTITUDE ADJUSTMENT — 5,200 feet. Add 1 tablespoon flour and bake at 375° for 5 minutes less.

A great way to serve a traditional flavor. Serve this moist cake with whipped topping for a holiday or everyday dessert.

Approximately 1 hr.

PUMPKIN PIE CAKE

1 package (18½ oz.) Pillsbury Applesauce Cake Mix

1¾ cups (1 lb. 2-oz. can) prepared pumpkin pie filling

½ cup water

3 eggs

Preheat oven to 350°. Blend cake mix, pumpkin pie mix, water and eggs until moistened. Beat as directed on package. Divide batter between two greased and floured 9-inch pie pans or pour into one 13x9-inch pan. Bake at 350° for 30 to 35 minutes or until done. Cool on wire rack before serving. To serve, top with prepared whipped topping or sweetened whipped cream. 13x9-INCH CAKE

Tip: *If pumpkin pie filling is not available, substitute 2 cups (1-lb. can) solid-pack pumpkin, 2½ teaspoons pumpkin pie spice and ½ cup firmly packed brown sugar. Prepare as directed above; reduce water to ¼ cup.

HIGH ALTITUDE ADJUSTMENT — 5,200 feet. Add a total of ⅔ cup water and 1 tablespoon flour. For Tip recipe, add a total of ⅓ cup water and 1 tablespoon flour. Bake at 375° for 30 to 40 minutes.

Approximately 40 min.

APPLE-CINNAMON UPSIDE-DOWN CAKE

1 teaspoon butter or margarine

½ cup apple jelly

1 can (11.7 oz.) Pillsbury Refrigerated Cinnamon Danish Rolls with Raisins

½ cup coconut

Preheat oven to 375°. Heat butter, jelly and icing from can of rolls in 8 or 9-inch round layer pan on top of range until bubbly. Sprinkle coconut over hot topping in pan. Separate dough into 8 rolls; arrange over hot topping. Bake at 375° for 25 to 30 minutes or until golden brown. Invert on serving plate. Serve warm. If desired, serve with whipped cream.

8 OR 9-INCH CAKE

Bananas are hidden inside a boat-shaped pastry. Easy for breakfast or dessert.

Approximately 25 min.

BANANA BOATS

¼ cup chopped salted peanuts

¼ cup flaked coconut

¼ cup powdered sugar

¼ teaspoon cinnamon

¼ teaspoon ground nutmeg

1 can (8 oz.) Pillsbury Refrigerated Quick Crescent Dinner Rolls

2 bananas, cut in half crosswise

1 tablespoon lemon juice

¼ cup maple syrup

¼ cup sifted powdered sugar

Preheat oven to 400°. Combine peanuts, coconut, ¼ cup powdered sugar, cinnamon and nutmeg. Separate crescent dough into 4 rectangles. Place rectangles of dough on ungreased cookie sheet. Sprinkle peanut mixture over each dough rectangle. Dip each banana half in lemon juice, then in maple syrup. Place each banana half on narrow end of dough rectangle and roll up ending with seam-side down. Pinch edges well to seal. Bake at 400° for 12 to 15 minutes or until golden brown. Sprinkle with ¼ cup powdered sugar while warm. Cut each roll into 4 pastries.   16 PASTRIES

Approximately 5 min.

QUICK CHEESECAKE FIX-UP

1 frozen prepared cheesecake (1 lb. 1 oz.)

1 cup (half of a 1-lb. can) prepared cherry pie filling*

Thaw cheesecake as directed on package. Spread top with pie filling. Cut into wedges to serve.   6 SERVINGS

Tips: *Other flavors pie filling can be used. Choose your favorite.

Leftovers can be stored, covered, in refrigerator for several days.

Remaining pie filling can be used as a topping for ice cream, cakes, waffles or pancakes.

Only four ingredients go into this very easy and delicious dessert. A super easy method shortens the time even more. Start it before you fix your meal.

Approximately 1 hr.

CHERRY CRISP

2 cups (one half pkg.) Pillsbury White Cake Mix*

2 cups (1 lb. 5-oz. can) prepared cherry pie filling

1 package Pillsbury Coconut Pecan or Coconut Almond Frosting Mix

½ cup butter or margarine, melted

Preheat oven to 350°. Grease and flour bottom and sides of 13x9-inch pan. Spread pie filling in pan. Sprinkle cake mix over cherries. Top with frosting mix. Pour melted butter evenly over mixture. Bake at 350° for 25 to 30 minutes until light golden brown. Cool before serving.

13x9-INCH DESSERT

Tip: *Store remaining cake mix tightly wrapped. To make a small cake, add 1 egg and ⅔ cup water. Bake in 8 or 9-inch square pan as directed on package.

Prepared tart shells and an especially easy filling take the time and effort out of these delicious tarts. Use your own creativity for other flavors.

Approximately 15 min.

PISTACHIO CREAM TARTLETS

1 package (3½ oz.) pistachio instant pudding mix

1 cup milk

1 cup frozen prepared whipped topping, thawed

1 package (6) prepared tart shells

Prepare pudding as directed on package, decreasing milk to 1 cup. When mixture has thickened, fold in whipped topping. Spoon into tart shells. If desired, garnish with chocolate jimmies.   6 SERVINGS

Tip: Other flavors of instant pudding mix and other garnishes can be used for the pistachio.

Belgian Dessert Waffles, opposite page

Waffles topped with fruit and ice cream do a new trick as a dessert. These are good for brunch, too!

Approximately 20 min.

BELGIAN DESSERT WAFFLES

1 package Pillsbury Yellow Cake Mix

1½ cups milk or light cream

4 eggs

½ teaspoon salt

Preheat waffle iron at medium heat. Lightly oil the waffle grid surface to prevent sticking. In large mixer bowl, combine cake mix, milk, eggs and salt. Blend and beat as directed on package. (Batter will be thick.) Pour about 1 cup batter (for a 9-inch waffle) in preheated waffle iron. Bake until waffle is golden brown, about 2 to 4 minutes. (Waffles will become crisper upon cooling.) Cool waffles on a wire rack. Stack sections of waffles and serve with whipped cream and fresh, canned or frozen fruit, drained if necessary.

6 LARGE WAFFLES

Tip: Leftover waffles can be wrapped tightly and refrigerated or frozen. If desired, reheat a few minutes in a toaster.

Pictured on page 57

Approximately 30 min.

PINEAPPLE CREAM PIE

1 9-inch baked pastry shell

½ cup (half of 3¾ oz. pkg.) instant pineapple cream pudding mix

½ cup milk

1 cup (half of 16-oz. can) prepared pineapple pie filling

In small mixing bowl, prepare pudding with milk as directed on package. Fold in pie filling. Spoon into pie shell. Chill 20 minutes or until serving time. If desired, top with whipped topping or sweetened whipped cream to serve.

6 SERVINGS

Tip: Filling can be prepared using entire package pudding mix, 1 cup milk and 1 entire can pie filling. Spoon half into pie shell. Chill remainder in bowl or serving dishes for another time.

Fluffy and light — this creamed filling goes into a speedy pie crust made with refrigerated cookies. Very elegant flavors.

Pictured on page 110

Approximately 50 min.

MOCHA PIE

½ chub (16 oz.) Pillsbury Refrigerated Fudge Nut Cookies

1 package (3½ oz.) chocolate whipped dessert mix

2 tablespoons sugar

2 to 3 teaspoons instant coffee

½ cup cold milk

½ cup cold water

½ cup dairy or imitation sour cream

Preheat oven to 375°. Slice cookie dough ⅛-inch thick. Line bottom and sides of greased and lightly sugared 8-inch pie pan, overlapping slightly. Bake at 375° for 8 to 10 minutes. Cool. In small mixer bowl, combine dry dessert mix, sugar and instant coffee. Add milk. Blend well on low speed. Beat on high speed 1 minute. Add water and beat 2 minutes more. Blend in sour cream. Chill while crust cools. Spoon into cooled cookie crust. Chill at least ½ hour before serving.

6 SERVINGS

This favorite dessert is only minutes away when crescent rolls double as a pastry dough. Serve them warm with cream or ice cream.

Pictured on page 110

Approximately 45 min.

SPICY APPLE CRESCENTS

½ cup sugar

1 teaspoon cinnamon

2 large apples, pared

1 can (8 oz.) Pillsbury Refrigerated Quick Crescent Dinner Rolls

¼ cup butter or margarine, melted

⅓ cup water

Preheat oven to 400°. Combine sugar and cinnamon; set aside. Cut each apple into 8 wedges. Separate dough into 8 triangles; cut each in half lengthwise, making 16 long thin triangles. Wrap each triangle around an apple wedge. Arrange in a 9-inch square pan; drizzle with butter. Sprinkle with sugar-cinnamon mixture and add water. Bake at 400° for 30 to 35 minutes. Serve warm with cream.

4 SERVINGS

Index